MW00777615

SEMIOTEXT(E) INTERVENTION SERIES

© La Fabrique Éditions, 2009.
This edition © Semiotext(e) 2021.

Published by Semiotext(e)
PO BOX 629, South Pasadena, CA 91031
www.semiotexte.com

Inside cover photograph: Hassane Mezine
Design: Hedi El Kholti

10 9 8 7 6 5 4 3 2 1

ISBN: 978-1-63590-146-7
Distributed by The MIT Press, Cambridge, Mass.
and London, England

Printed in the United States of America

Sadri Khiari

The Colonial Counter-Revolution in France

From de Gaulle to Sarkozy

Translated by Ames Hodges

semiotext(e)
intervention
series □ 31

Contents

Introduction: Giving Life Back to   13
Those Who Came Before

1. The Proof of Social Races Is in Their Struggle!   25

2. The Republic Is a Liar   49

3. Why We Should Hate Charles de Gaulle   67

4. First Racial Skirmishes in the Heart of France   86

5. From Marronage to Jihad: The Metamorphoses   111
of Indigenous Power

6. How the Strategic Unity of White Power Was Built   145

7. Working-Class Neighborhoods: The Epicenter of   181
the Struggle of the Social Races

8. A New Phase in the Colonial Counter-Revolution   207

Heading into the Waves...   226

Notes   241

I'd like to express all my gratitude to my friends Sonia Al-Barbecha, Hakim Bouzellouf, and Houria Bouteldja for their critical revisions of this text. Thank you as well to Eric Hazan for his belief.

For my sister Samira

"In what I tell you, there's the almost-true, the sometimes-true, and the half-true. That's what telling a life is like, braiding all of that like one plaits the white Indies currant's hair to make a hut. And the true-true comes out of that braid. And Sophie, you can't be scared of lying if you want to know everything."

—Patrick Chamoiseau, *Texaco*, 1997 [1992]

"All right, gentlemen, I'm taking over now."
—Jonathan Jackson

Introduction

Giving Life Back to Those Who Came Before

> *"'Our' generation, therefore, like the generation before us, tried to give our children all that we had never had. And sometimes forgot, or sometimes lost sight of the fact—again, paraphrasing Andy—that the battle our forebears fought with 'the limits' gave them the strength to raise us to be men and women.* This *strength is our real inheritance, and it must not be betrayed—certainly not for the Yankee-Western mess of pottage."*
>
> —James Baldwin, *The Evidence of Things Not Seen*[1]

We know Abdelmalek Sayad's famous saying, "To exist is to exist politically."[2] It has been quoted many times. It expresses life in society in a simple way. The social bond is political. Many have said it before him. But Sayad was not talking about Human Beings. He was talking Immigrants. He was speaking about Immigration, about immigration from the colonies. He was speaking about us: blacks, Arabs, Muslims. Those of us who have been present in France for a long time or arrived more recently. "First, second, third generation..." French. Non-French. We who do not exist, we who are not supposed to exist, and yet who EXIST EXTREMELY. Sayad speaks of this distortion of existence: *not* to exist politically is *not* to exist. French society refuses our existence; consequently, it refuses our *political* existence. The Republic refuses our political existence; consequently, it refuses our *existence*. In France, supposedly, there are only French people and foreigners passing through. All of them free, equal, and indistinct. Unless they fail to respect the Law, of course. The Republic does not want to see us and does not want us to be seen. The Republic can't stomach us. It doesn't hear us. Marianne-the-White is deaf. All she hears is her rooster. Because seeing us, hearing us, stomaching us would mean seeing the indigenous,[3] smelling their stench. It would mean knowing its own negation: the Republic exists through its indigenous. Today's indigenous were yesterday's colonized or the slaves of the day before. Equality is the opposite of equality. Citizenship is the denial of citizenship. Fraternity is contempt. The nation is the race.

For everyone's peace of mind, it would be better if we did not exist. Or only as a concept. A "problem," for example, there's a nice concept. The "problem of immigration." The "black question." Or the "banlieues,"[4] another abstraction to talk about us without talking about us. The nice humanist would say "the Other," as in, "We must accept the Other," "tolerate them." If it's a white person on the left, they will talk about "scapegoats": "The vile right-wing government uses immigrants as scapegoats to turn workers away from their legitimate struggles." A "scapegoat" does not act and therefore does not exist. Scapegoat yourself! Otherwise, they will talk about "scarecrows": "Fascists use immigration as a scarecrow," etc. A "scarecrow" is scary but does not act or exist any more than a bale of hay. Scarecrow yourself! In sum, the anti-racist left says this: only the racist *illusion* makes one believe that Arabs and blacks exist in France. It is also what is meant by the well-known "anti-racist" argument: "Unlike what the Right claims, immigration is not increasing." Good people of France, take assurance in the fact that immigrants exist no more today than they did in the past and they continue to vote for the Left!

The white people on the left also have a soft spot for "undocumented immigrants," probably because they do not exist at all. And because to exist, even a little bit, they have to ask the Left for help. Undocumented immigrants do not exist at all because in order to exist they must threaten to put an end to their own existence. The proof that I exist, they say, is that I am dying. And they stop eating. And the Left finds a good excuse to denounce the Right: "Give them papers so they will eat and stop existing!" Because if they get their papers, they stop being undocumented, and if, as undocumented immigrants they did not exist *at all*, once they get their papers, they *do not* exist, that's all. Which is a form of progress. Undocumented immigrants do not exist at all because they are not even foreigners, since the law clearly states what foreigners look like and they do not meet this definition. They are outlaws, delinquents, illegal immigrants, *irregular*. A lot of terms for those who do not exist. They are irregular humans. "Regularization for all undocumented immigrants!" says the left-wing militant who leans strongly to the left. That way undocumented immigrants will become *regular humans*.

It reminds me of the times of slavery when white abolitionists believed that relationships of force—between whites—did not yet allow for anything more than asking to give slaves the right to wear shoes or a shirt. In 1799, the Left in Great Britain won what was a great victory at the time: from that point onward, according to the new law, deported Africans in the holds of the ships that were transporting them to America would each have eight square feet at their disposal instead of five to six square feet![5] It must be progress, since the Right, if it knew about it, would have probably suggested they be vacuum-packed to keep them from spoiling.

I will not deny my sarcasm here. White people on the far left are not only asking for the regularization of all undocumented immigrants. They are also demanding the right to vote for immigrants. That way, they will be able to vote... for the Left. Because in their eyes, immigrants only exist if they are on the left. If they have a nature, their nature is the same: to be on the left. They must be *loyal* to the Left. The left brings them into the world as a regular human and might one day grant them the right to vote; how then could they be on the right? "The necessities of the case," as the great abolitionist leader William Lloyd Garrison declared, "require not only that you should behave as well as the whites, but better than the whites."[6] Incidentally, if immigrants are not on the left, it means they are on the right. They cannot be themselves. They never exist for themselves. France is the Right and the Left; the world is the Right and the Left; if immigrants claim to be themselves, they return to the void; they no longer exist. They were miserable ghosts, victims, scapegoats, proof that the Right-is-bad. They become another kind of specter: "communitarians," "Islamists," "anti-white racists," and the list goes on!... In sum, for the Right, we are muscle; for the Left, we are on the left.

So, we don't exist. We exist *through Them*. Which comes down to the same thing. We do not exist because we *must not* exist. We do not exist because recognizing our existence would mean recognizing our *political* existence and recognizing our political existence would mean recognizing that They do not want this political existence. It would mean recognizing that politics must happen without us, outside of us, behind us, through us, over our heads, but never *with* us. Maybe, if anything, *against* us. That would be tolerated. If anything! But the phrase does not hold. When politics is against us, it is never *really against* us. It is against the workers, the popular masses, the socially excluded; the Right uses racism to make things difficult for the Left, that is all. We are not even victims, but indirect victims, collateral damage from another fight. Scapegoats, they say.

But also this: recognizing our political existence would mean recognizing our struggles; the ones we lead for ourselves and that disrupt France. It would mean recognizing that not everything filters through them. That the conflict between the "right" and the "left," between "Progress" and "reaction," between "Modernity" and "obscurantism," or between the "bourgeoisie" and the "proletariat," is not universally accepted. Recognizing our political existence would lead them to this horrific discovery: in contemporary society, the social tie is also *racial*. The word *race* is scary; it stinks. Tell them that society itself stinks! And that word is scary not because it was used to keep blacks in slavery and subjugate people from the colonies at the expense of multiple genocides, but because it was used for whites who were in a rush to exterminate other whites.

The social tie is racial. Which means that politics are racial. Society is racial, which means that the social tie occurs around racial inequality. Politics are racial, which means that racial inequality is the struggle of the dominated social race against the dominant social race. And *vice versa*. The social power relations that are being woven in that confrontation are political relations of power and these political relations of power are power relations between social races.

WE EXIST BECAUSE WE EXIST POLITICALLY AND WE EXIST POLITICALLY BECAUSE WE ARE THE OBJECTS AND SUBJECTS OF THE POLITICAL RELATIONS OF POWER BETWEEN RACES.

They don't want to hear about that.

And quite often, neither do we... We *believe we exist* by seizing the white gaze. Besides, it's difficult not to do this. We experience that abysmal shame of being proud of speaking just like them. Sometimes we experience the incommensurable joy of having conned them. We try to please them only to betray them. Maroons to the tips of our fingers, we will flee when we need to flee. Since we are nothing, let's be cunning. I say "Yes, Bwana," and once your back is turned, I plant my knife in it. Resistance. "Whites, masters of the language? Masters—unhappy in any case—of definitions, when beginning with a point chosen by them and which they call the West, they divide the entire rest of the world into Near East, East, Far East."[7] Our brother—their declared enemy—Jean Genet wrote this. He was powerless, as we are, to rupture words simply with words. Language, thought, and "science" belong to them. No truth is true without the stick that comes with it. For words, we will use venomous ones. But how can we completely get rid of the categories of the white world that submerge us? Genet, once again: "Finally, every young black American who writes is searching for himself and testing himself, and sometimes he recognizes, at his very center, in his own heart, a white man he must annihilate."[8] Stokely Carmichael, the founder of Black Power, says the same thing: "We shall have to struggle for the right to create our own terms through which to define ourselves and our relationship to the society, and to have these terms recognized. This is the first necessity of a free people, and the first right that any oppressor must suspend."⁹ How can we *think* outside of them? Personally, I have no idea. I suppose it will only be through our struggles—against the institutions that produce words—that we will be able to produce our own categories. Not in libraries. Or not only in libraries. This book, in any case, is not free. It is at most an attempted escape. I like the prisoners who dig endless tunnels with a simple aluminum spoon. They don't exist either. Or rather, they exist when they are digging. Let's dig!

My own spoon is the Movement of the Indigenous of the Republic.¹⁰ It told me that I existed, and, with others, I am transmitting that message. The goal of the pages that follow is to say that we exist. They are stammering. "Stammering in this case is invaluable because it keeps us from rigid and mechanical certainties."¹¹ Through a stammering analysis of the web of the racial relations of power that have developed over the past several decades leading up to the November 2005 revolt and the election of Sarkozy, this book says that we have existed for a multitude of time. That marronage and insurrections under slavery in America, the uprisings and wars of our colonized ancestors, the protests, strikes, and riots of immigrants and their children are one of the truths of their existence. And of ours. Those Who Came Before changed the world just as the world had changed them: they changed France just like France had changed them. Their existence is visible everywhere in contemporary France, even though their bodies disappeared a long time ago, and even though the Republic blurs the view and claims that this existence is simply an optical illusion. "France," says France, "has always been and will always be France." It doesn't matter that we don't really know what prescription to get for our new glasses! Let's break the distorting lenses that the Republic has stuck on our noses and see for ourselves.

We will see that Those Who Came Before existed and continue to exist. The "duty to remember" does not just mean we have the duty to say that they were here and that they suffered, to show the roads they built and to cry over their lost traditions. It does not just mean asking that they have the right to a few lines in school textbooks, a 1/4-inch square rather than a 3/16-inch square of white paper and maybe an old photo. And even less creating a museum in Vincennes. It means affirming their political existence. Narrating their struggles and learning them by heart is not bad, but it is just a narrative. We must affirm the political efficacy of their struggles and of their resistances, show that Those Who Came Before not only made cars but also the political relations of power that were crystalized in the institutions, the ways of thinking, and the social relations that are constantly active in today's political relations of power, that move and are transfigured before our eyes, and that transform the society in which we live. Bringing Those Who Came Before back to life of course means joining in their struggles, continuing them—following and prolonging them—and refuting their inexistence and ours. Not to open the eyes of whites, finally, but to shut the eyes of white supremacy, definitively. Bringing Those Who Came Before back to life is our emancipation.

This book is simply an act of existence. In other words, it is an act of Dignity.

1

The Proof of Social Races Is in Their Struggle!

"What, then, is the nature of this vertiginous space that—in America and throughout the Christian West—separates Man (the basis of Humanism!) and the black? It is still obvious that, as a whole, all of the laws of which Man is so proud are not set up for the black. They are even set up against him."
—Jean Genet, 1971

"Decolonization is the encounter between two congenitally antagonistic forces that in fact owe their singularity to the kind of reification secreted and nurtured by the colonial situation."
—Frantz Fanon, *The Wretched of the Earth*

I am not interested in the biological question (do races exist in nature?). Besides, racists are not really interested in it either. Whatever science says on the subject, they remain convinced about the existence of races. And I am not concerned with moral, anthropologizing or psychologizing reflections on racism as the perverse and deadly expression of the relation to the Other. They delight those obsessed with meditating on the prepucecular moment; they are of no pertinence for activists. These reflections leave politics and history to return to a supposed *eternal nature* of Humankind, its deviations, its aberrations, or its pathologies. Or they refocus explanations of racism on representations and the imaginary. Ideology, false consciousness, and other bad influences become the ultimate truth of social reality. According to these paradigms, racism could perhaps transform through history and peoples, shift its target or manifest under particular forms (religious intolerance, nationalism, culturalism, biologism, etc.) but in the final analysis it is the avatar of an invariant, the fundamental heterophobia of Humans. The unstated postulate of these theories is that racism is engendered by real dissimilarities and by the heterogeneity specific to humanity and not by the unequal social relations that valorize or produce and fetishize these disparities. From this perspective, "anti-racism" comes down to promoting "tolerance," "broadening people's minds," modifying representations, shaking up norms, teaching human diversity so that Humans can accept the Other in its Difference. It is no longer a question of politics—

of power relations, of struggles to shake up or topple the state—but of moral pedagogy.

Really, who cares whether *hatred of the Other* is universal and timeless, or close to it!

The fact that phenomena similar to white racism may have existed in other guises in India, in Japan, in certain regions of Africa, in the Arab-Islamic world, or elsewhere, does not say anything about the relations of domination that the white planet has been exerting on other peoples for centuries. There is no use expounding on the generality—and the reciprocal contamination—of forms of essentializing, naturalizing, belittling, rejecting, despising, not tolerating, or fearing of the Other that accompany the spread of racism and most, if not all, relations between individuals or groups of individuals in unequal societies, or even simply the relations between different communities and societies. White supremacy only exists in its historical specificities. Racism is just one—ideological—mode of existence of the *struggle between social races*. So far as we are concerned, we are not interested in knowing if races exist or not outside of the social and political relations that wove them through a particular space-time. Our exclusive concern is this question: what defines the social relations that simultaneously produce and oppose hierarchically ranked social groups that think of themselves and oppose themselves as races, delimited by imagined and reified differences? Through what forms of social logic and political confrontation does the illusion of races denounced by the anti-racists refer to a very concrete social reality, the struggle of social races?

Speaking of *social races* means first pointing out the peculiarity of the social tie mediated by these differences. It means understanding the modalities through which the social tie has taken the form of a specific social polarization that delimits *statutory groups* in racial terms. By which I mean social groups whose hierarchically-ranked relations express predominantly *political* apparatuses of allocation and constraint, and the imposition of norms and other *symbolic* distinctions, in other words, a more or less explicitly institutionalized *status* that does not necessarily fall under the economic order. Statutory groups are therefore distinct from Marxist social classes. Or, more precisely, in their first forms (castes, estates, ...) classes were also statutory groups in as much as they were intertwined in relations of "personal dependence" (*Capital*) that characterized all spheres of social life and were therefore *directly* political. In the pre-capitalist world, the dominant classes were immediately constitutive of political power and as such they claimed part of the riches produced by the dominated classes. "The hierarchical structure of land ownership, and the armed bodies of retainers associated with it, gave the nobility power over the serfs."[12] In egalitarian capitalist democracy, the state has become (relatively) autonomous, classes are no longer directly implied, and the extortion of wealth occurs through the logic of Capital. As we will see, the constitution of races, principally characterized by their respective statuses in the political and symbolic order, occurs through a completely different development.

Just as Capital produces classes and Patriarchy produces genders, Global-European Colonialism produces races. It constitutes a mechanism of differentiation and hierarchical ranking of humanity between one pole, defined according to race, that is granted invisible or manifest privileges, and a second racial pole whose subjection to all sorts of invisible or manifest violence guarantees the privileges of the dominant pole. The existence of a racialized individual is determined here by their racial status, that is to say, by belonging to a group defined as an inferior or superior race. The first pole is the white world, for which the political dimension is constituted by White Power (*pouvoir*), a power more often institutionalized than disorganized. The second pole is the indigenous world, for which the political dimension is Indigenous Political Power (*puissance*), a power that is more often virtual, inorganic and split up than it is institutionalized. Being white does not necessarily mean having white skin; it means being an integral part of the white world and being recognized as such. It means benefitting from statutory privileges guaranteed by the state. Being indigenous does not necessarily mean having black skin or lowering one's eyes; it means existing socially as a condition of possibility and of realization of white privilege.

Speaking about social races therefore also means highlighting the unity of a historical process, in this case this relation of domination/resistance inscribed in the same historical continuum that was gradually globalized in the form of the enslavement of blacks, colonization, then the different forms of apartheid and segregation that the descendants of slaves and of colonized peoples were continually subjected to and against which they still resist. For it is indeed in the *colonization of the world*, a concrete historical form espoused by economic, political and cultural globalization from the beginning of European expansion in Africa and the "discovery" of the Americas that we must see the production of social races, that is to say the emergence of white supremacy or the structuring of a global political field articulated around the confrontation between White Power (*pouvoir*) and Indigenous Political Power (*puissance*).

Let us first clarify this point: there are different forms of colonization. The conquests of Alexander the Great or the different Muslim or Chinese empires do not have much to do with European colonial globalization, rooted in particular in the European upheavals following the Renaissance with the progressive expansion of Capital and the jarring creation of nation-states. Not all territorial expansion or oppression of peoples was as racializing as European colonization. The same is true for slavery, which is not in itself racializing. The generic notion of slavery is in fact misleading, as it suggests a social tie of the same nature between master and slave in societies that are often incomparable. Being the "owner" of a human being has absolutely different meanings in the framework of communities where "property" as form refers to different social logics and relations. In its beginnings, the establishment of slavery relations in America was rooted in practices that had been customary in Southern Europe for several centuries.[13] Originally, the enslavement of Indians and blacks was not more racialist than slavery in Antiquity, the Arab slave trade, or slavery as it was practiced by almost all the societies we know of, including African societies. Thus, in the Arab world, the peoples of Sub-Saharan Africa were not enslaved at first because they were black. However, as it developed as a moment of the contemporary colonial process, the *nature* of slavery *progressively changed*. The deportation of blacks and their enslavement can only be qualified as racial inasmuch as they participated in the establishment of social relations that instituted a hierarchy between a statutory group defined as white and another defined as black (before encompassing all "indigenous" people). From this point of view, in the new colonial context, slavery *completely fabricated* the social reality that constitutes race. Neither races nor racism predated it. As James Baldwin expressed it perfectly, "I say to 'become' White, for they had not been White before their arrival, any more than I, in Africa, had been Black. I had been part of a tribe and a language and a nation."[14] And he added, "The 'European'—a catchall term, referring, really, to the dooms of Capital, Christianity, and Color— *became* White, and the African *became* Black—for commercial reasons."[15] Since the colonial relation is also a relation of resistance to colonization, we could supplement Baldwin's statements by adding: blacks are a creation of whites and of black *resistance*. Whites are a *creation* of whites, just as they are the product of black resistance. Black is not a color; it's a social relation. Muslims today are not necessarily followers of the Muslim faith; they are a social relation. And of course, white is not a color; it is a social relation, a relationship of struggle, and a political relation.

Over the course of its existence, the transatlantic slave trade was a major component of those processes in which capitalist accumulation, the creation of nation-states, European colonial expansion and the construction of white-Christian-European-supremacist identity were blended and conflated. Several studies have highlighted these structural relations. I will not revisit this except to emphasize one component for which in-depth examination could reveal the modernity of the racialization of social relations. The most convincing hypothesis seems to be that, in fact, far from being an archaism that persists in the world of individual freedom, equality and democracy, social races are instead one of its ways of being. The pre-capitalist statutory groups that existed prior to the advent of modern states and nations were dissolved in the very movement through which racial statutory groups were formed in the recomposed and hierarchical space of colonization. Although nothing was yet settled during the Renaissance, it was nonetheless the moment when European expansion started into the Americas and Africa, which were linked by the slave trade, and with the crises and changes that the principal Western European centers underwent. At their heart, the distinctions drawn during Greek Antiquity between civilized peoples and barbarians were reinterpreted to make sense of the reclassifications of the social pyramid. They get introduced into, absorb, or even progressively replace the medieval or feudal statutory divisions. The latter maintained a certain power for a long time, notably on a symbolic level, but they corresponded less and less to the real structuring of social forces that were being shaken, in particular by the accelerated development of the bourgeois classes and the strengthening of secular states to the detriment of the clergy. The hierarchy of estates gradually faded, overthrown by the democratic revolutions of the eighteenth and nineteenth centuries. On top of it was superimposed another statutory hierarchy opposing the rich, urbanized populations who were more or less participants in political authority and distinguished by "civility" from the subaltern urban classes, associated with the same naturalness, or more honestly savagery, as rural populations, regardless of whether they be wealthy, members of the clergy, or military nobility.[16] The racialization of slavery relations in the Americas may seem at first like the product of the *exporting* to the colonies of these social, political and ideological relations of which the metamorphosis accompanied the gestation of modern society. But through a kind of historical contraction, it is also the product of the reactivation of *pre*-feudal slavery relations in the heart of *post*-feudal European society. The unstable and often contradictory forms of norms, codes, and laws through which the social races were progressively established—and only admitted rarely and belatedly—testify to those historical overlaps.

However, beyond the diverse and shifting responses of the different codifying bodies (states, the church, and others), the colonial slave system was constituted in the end as a statutory hierarchy with the deported African slaves at the bottom and at the top, the Christian-Europeans who would soon define themselves as whites, while "slave" and "black" grew to become synonymous.

In the meantime, a large proportion of the Native Americans. The survivors, whose subordination had been established, were not considered apt for the harshest labor. The church also prohibited their enslavement, preferring the euphemism of "forced labor." The growing infiltration of the Portuguese and Spanish into West Africa, the relative ease with which they could acquire black slaves, the intensification of the Arabic trans-Saharan slave trade no doubt also contributed to the fact that, from the middle of the fifteenth century onward, slave relations became increasingly characterized by the almost *exclusive* and *massive* character of black slavery that favored the *confusion between the condition of being a slave and color*, in other words, the racialization of slavery.[17] The way was then opened to the opposite process, the *independence of color from the slave condition*. Color became the foundation of social status, independent of the place the individual occupied in economic production.

Although it was already strongly anchored in everyday life, this evolution is perceptible in the ambiguities of the slave codes that officially assigned individuals their respective places in the racial hierarchy. Promulgated after the end of the seventeenth century, these codes circumscribed statutory groups defined by race.[18] The first *Code Noir* (1685) that regulated the status of slaves in the French Antilles and in Guyana did not explicitly use the notion of "race," as its use with human beings had not yet been established, but its aim was clear: it did not simply codify the relation between a simple working body and its owner, but a race relation. Officially, as Françoise Vergès explains, the Code Noir was "founded on a distinction established not between whites and blacks, but between individuals who are *born* free and individuals who are *not* free or have *become* free (through emancipation)."[19] However, the author explains, "the dividing line is not only between those who are *born* free and those who are *not* free, or who have *become* free, but also between whites, who are free by birth, and blacks, who are slaves by nature."[20] The status that it regulated simultaneously associates and dissociates social positions according to production and color. In 1724, a second version of the Code Noir was enacted for Louisiana. Henceforth, according to Danielle Lochak, "the 'racial' component of slavery appears more explicitly: the terms *black slave* appear in the preamble and the term *white* is used several times."[21] In particular, the Code prohibits marriages between blacks and whites. It also notes "that slaves can only be witnesses if no *whites* are available."[22] The dissociation between the status of blacks and the status of slaves was made manifest in Article 52, which stipulated that "freed slaves and free blacks cannot receive any donations or inheritance from whites." Even once they have "become free," blacks remain black; they are not equal to whites.

Quite often the "birth" of racism is situated between the end of the eighteenth century and the beginning of the nineteenth, when the premises of biological racism appeared. This approach implies that the racial distinction is a fundamentally ideological form. However, this periodization holds meaning. Not as much because naturalist ideology and scientism invented biological differences between human beings at the time, but more certainly because this period created the conditions of a fundamental dissociation between socio-economic status and racial status. Races were born. And the oppressed race could henceforth be politically incarnated as such, as a racial political force, as a racial power.

I have already highlighted the fact that the racial social tie is constituted through a double movement of racial oppression and resistance to that oppression. As awful as it was, the Code Noir that regulated and codified the status of blacks also aimed to define the legitimate forms of repression to use against them. However, it also reacted to slave resistance, to pressure from freed slaves, and to demands by people of mixed-race, fueled by the individual arbitrariness of whites, which had been allowed until then by the lack of all legislation.[23] From that perspective, the juridical and ideological crystallization of racial statuses sanctioned by the Code Noir appeared to express the development of the struggle of social races. If we wanted to give a date to the day racial relations "matured," I would have to choose the day Toussaint Louverture proclaimed the freedom of Saint-Domingue, renaming it Haiti. By establishing itself as a political power, as a state, the black social race gave full political content and form to racial resistance for the first time in the history of colonization. Marx asserted that "the form of the dictatorship of the proletariat had finally been found" in the Paris Commune and opened the period of proletarian revolution, in other words of its historical topicality, its *possibility*. We could say the same about Black Power in Haiti, that it opened the period of decolonial revolution. To those who would say that Black Power in Haiti was simply the product of the French Revolution, I would answer that the Paris Commune was simply the product of the German invasion. There is certainly a historical convergence between 1789 and the anti-slavery revolution in Saint-Domingue, but it is not situated exactly where French ethnocentrism would put it. The link between the two events can be found in the juncture between the historical trajectory of racial relations and slave struggles, and the historical trajectory of capitalism and the bourgeois democratic movement. But this juncture should not be seen as some virtuous rapport between these two processes that would have led to the abolition of slavery via the expansion of humanism and the Enlightenment. The articulation is rather to be found in the perverse relation that, while emancipating European society from pre-capitalist statutory hierarchies (such as the estates), it also emancipated race relations from those hierarchies. In other words, from then on, race relations were no longer inscribed in the network of statutory relations of more or less feudal origin, but in the growing network of bourgeois democratic relations. More precisely, the advent of bourgeois democracy gives rise to races. "The history of the West," as Domenico Losurdo writes on this question, "is faced with a paradox that can be understood based on the history of its current guiding country [...]. The clear line of demarcation between whites on the one hand and blacks and redskins on the other encouraged the development of relations of equality within the white community."[24] This statement also means that "the development of relations of equality within the white community" supported the crystallization of specifically racial social relations. In his analysis of the genesis of racism, G.M. Frederickson notes that "to become the ideological basis of a social order," racism had to "be clearly disassociated from traditionalist conceptions of social hierarchy. In a society in which inequality based on birth was the norm for everyone from king down to peasant, ethnic slavery and ghettoization were special cases of a general pattern—very special in some ways—but still not radical exceptions to the hierarchical premise. Paradoxical as it may seem, the rejection of hierarchy as the governing principle of social and political organization, and its replacement by the aspiration for equality in this world as well as in the eyes of God, had to occur before racism could come to full flower."[25] And he adds, in the same vein, " As has been suggested, modernization or "becoming modern" was a precondition for the overtly racist regimes. […] The norm of common citizenship and equal rights in modern nation-states could turn strong prejudices into systematic exclusions of a kind that could be justified only if the excluded were regarded as less than fully human or, at best, as inherently immature and thus incapable of assuming the responsibilities of adulthood."[26]

At the moment when the republic inflicted a decisive defeat to the harshest forms of aristocratic counterrevolution, when it surmounted monarchist and imperial reactions and overcame the opposition of slave traders, bankers, and white colonists who were against abolition, it definitively broke the chains binding blacks to slavery but consecrated the chains of blackness. With democratization, "negro" was no longer a synonym of "slave." The negro race was no longer the "class" of slaves. From that point on, you could be a "dirty negro" and get lynched even if you were a free farmer, a craftsman, or a lawyer. It even became possible for black people to gain a certain repute and have institutional responsibilities, which was useful to placate some of their recriminations, and yet remain "dirty negroes." In other words, democratization did not mean that blacks were freed from racial social relations; rather, it meant the racial social relations were freed from slavery and other pre-democratic forms.[27] Liberated thanks to democracy, racial relations would finally be able to exist for themselves and spread to the entire planet, opposing whites to all the non-whites that the French Republic would call "indigenous" (and that it now calls "diversity"). The estates are dead, long live races!

However, the principles of capitalist democracy are individual freedom and political equality. Races negate it but are also inseparable from it. Bourgeois modernity, which was established at the turn of the eighteenth and nineteenth centuries, developed at the crossroads of two contradictory yet complementary movements: the freedom of individuals from the constraints of statutory hierarchies that were essential to the affirmation of the modern state and to the flourishing of capital, and the imperial expansion that was just as necessary. It was out of the question that races could be expressed as such, as a form of statutory hierarchy linked to imperial expansion, and yet they had to be expressed, or rather, they had to be produced! The great colonization movement that stretches from the middle of the nineteenth century until World War II continually produced race in the form of the *indigénat* (according to the meaning the term acquired in French colonial legislation). Yet colonial states could not directly identify themselves as race states (it is in fact very clear in French colonial law, which only rarely draws on the notion of race even though it was present in every mind).[28] For a time, however, the ideology of biological racial differences provided a "scientific" foundation to white statutory domination, enabling its "justification" without any excessive disruption of the egalitarian democratic principle. But contemporary "neocolonialism" would resolve the equation even more efficiently. Although the new forms of "indirect" colonization are certainly the product of indigenous struggles (and of their limitations), they also express the constitutive paradoxes of an inseparably egalitarian and imperial democratic capitalism. As opposed to the colonial dictatorships of previous centuries, indirect forms of domination are perfectly adapted to the deep logic of contemporary society, which depersonalizes social actors or, more generally, subordinates them to impersonal or abstract social logics. In fact, in all areas of social life, the different apparatuses of domination are increasingly indirect. Up to a certain point, they dispense with the immediate constraints exercised by individuals, groups, or states. The strict institutionalized boundaries of statutory groups and of their hierarchies are no longer always necessary for their reproduction. Individuals can be defined as free, equal, and fraternal, and indeed they are that way on certain levels, which is one of the mechanisms through which they are dominated. With the dissolution of colonial empires and the appearance of new forms of empire, although still quite real, racial polarization has grown blurred and is now reconfigured through disparate places and indirect means. Racial polarization is masked by the multiple, opaque mediations through which it is constituted, by the proliferation of hierarchies and categories that are used to say and camouflage races at the same time, and by the relative permeability of statutory racial groups. Racial relations have gone underground; globally, they are reproduced mainly through the contemporary forms of inter-state domination and the contradictory mediation of new, "independent" nation-states. Imperial oppression and popular resistance to this oppression also occur via patterns of emigration from the old colonies towards the imperialist centers, building a population of "internal colonized" peoples. People on the left who "like" immigrants believe it is in good taste to quote Sayad. However, they never mention his fundamental position: "Emigration brings to mind the precedent of colonization, just as the situation of emigrants is reminiscent of that of colonized people; in a sense colonization survives through emigration, which prolongs it."[29]

At the heart of the imperialist metropolis, writes Etienne Balibar, the emigrant thus becomes the "new name of race." An elusive, impersonal, and abstract "invisible hand" of racism, generated by the racialized structure of global society refracted at the heart of dominant states, works tirelessly for the perpetuation of race relations, often independently of concrete actors. This is how we can interpret Angela Davis's statement that "the varieties of racism that define our present era are so deeply embedded in institutional structures and so complexly mediated that they now appear to be detached from the persons they harm with their violence."[30] And in the same way, we could add, they appear detached from the actors of this violence. A few years prior, the theorists of Black Power had expressed this process in terms of "institutional racism," which they distinguished from "individual racism." "By 'racism' we mean the predication of decisions and policies on considerations of race for the purpose of subordinating a racial group and maintaining control over that group. [...] Racism is both overt and covert. It takes two, closely related forms: individual whites acting against individual blacks, and acts by the total white community against the black community. We call these individual racism and institutional racism. The first consists of overt acts by individuals, which cause death, injury or the violent destruction of property. This type can be recorded by television cameras; it can frequently be observed in the process of commission. The second type is less overt, far more subtle, less identifiable in terms of *specific* individuals committing the acts. But it is no less destructive of human life. The second type originates in the operation of established and respected forces in the society, and thus receives far less public condemnation than the first type."[31]

Such largely anonymous racism renders obsolete the juridical or other use of explicitly racialist categories, or of transparently discriminatory categories. It even basks in the apology of "interracial marriage" and "mixed-race progeny." But racial hybridity does not dissolve races, just as the subterfuge of the "middle class" does not dissolve social classes. The mechanisms that delimit races are now developing around a number of categories that pertain to faith, culture, tradition, science, and the law, but they are also expressed in forms that might seem unrelated at first glance, and unrelated to any willful racial distinction. The dominant race defines itself as Christian, European, white, civilized, Western, universal, democratic, liberal, rational, secular, feminist, antiracist, a fan of the satirical weekly *Charlie-Hebdo*, hailing from the world's richest countries, pureblood national, resident of the wealthiest areas, NATO member, etc. The dominated race is defined as savage, barbarian, negroid, indigenous, Oriental, immigrant, illegal, thuggish, developing, from the least developed countries (LDC), the minority candidate, Muslim, terrorist, polygamous, from the inner city, etc. I am purposefully borrowing from what appear to be motley categories. In reality, these multiple definitions refer to the same reality: the racial polarization stemming from the colonial partitioning, the categories used to demarcate races without necessarily designating them as such, and the institutions through which the struggle of social races is organized. Indirect and impersonal forms of racial oppression, expressed in indirect and impersonal terms, have partially replaced more manifest forms of racial oppression.

Ultimately, as Stokely Carmichael and Charles V. Hamilton explain, the "acts by the total white community" and " the operation of established and respected forces in the society" that produce institutional racism constitute white political power (*puissance*) as it is produced through racial social logics and condensed in the state. That state is the modern, centralized, bureaucratic, national state that began with the emergence of absolutist monarchies in Europe and that was chiseled down, defeudalized, and democratized with the bourgeois revolutions of the end of the eighteenth century. It is the state that acts as the political mediation between individuals and social groups, and that incarnates the process through which political ties become autonomous, that is, that process of (relative) dissociation between the different dimensions of the social bond and its appropriation by a bureaucratic apparatus. This state constitutes the central body that reproduces institutional racism and the statutory differentiation between races.

Racial social relations in France are the product of the particular way that the French state was constituted as inscribed within this global history.

They are the product of the contemporary inscription of France in relations of domination on a global scale. The French state is continually weaving and reweaving the framework of race relations. Race relations continually weave and reweave the framework of the state. The Republic is the product of the racial social relations. Contrary to what people often believe, racism is not a malfunction in the Republic; it is the *normal* operation of the Republic. *The Republic is White Power.*

2

The Republic Is a Liar

"We aspire not to equality but to domination. The country of a foreign race must become once again a country of serfs, of agricultural laborers, or industrial workers. It is not a question of eliminating the inequalities among men but of widening them and making them into a law."
—Ernst Renan, *Intellectual and Moral Reform of France*, 1871

"I was crushed by the concept of France."
—Jean Genet, 1983

I think the French Revolution lied. Not entirely, oh no! Its most ardent fans should not worry! I myself admit to a certain fondness for the revolutionaries who cut their king in half. Actually, it should happen more often. And yet, in reality—not in the ideals held by its most radical partisans—the

French revolution was not the revolution of equality that it claimed to be. Or, to be more precise, it only instituted a certain form of equality. This is now a fairly banal statement. The suppression of the feudal order, which occurred almost naturally, confirmed their de facto disintegration. Many scholars have also noted that the juridical equality between individuals was, at least in part, a ploy that both enabled and dissimulated production of the characteristic inequalities of the capitalist mode of production. Others have highlighted the fact that the Revolution did not call into question either gender oppression nor slavery (abolished in 1794, reinstated by Napoleon, and then definitely banned by the Second Republic in 1848). In sum, supposedly, the Revolution did not reach its full democratic and egalitarian potential. The idea then would be to complete it, to enable "formal," strictly juridical equality to become "real" social equality, and for reality to correspond to the law, acts to coincide with discourse, and the Republic to align with the republican myth. For this, the republican social pact would need to be truly social. Republican citizenship would need to be really civic, and the "sovereignty of the people" would need to be actually sovereign and for the people. Today, everyone bemoans the fact that this prospect seems more remote than ever, that the social pact is disintegrating, that the notion of citizenship is being emptied, and that the Republic is less and less republican. Yet it means forgetting that the republican pact, as it was historically established, and not without contradictions, is also a national "ethnic" pact that is inseparable from the internal competition of the white world and a racial pact that is inseparable from the imperial expansion of the French state.

Let us clarify what the notion of the "republican pact" means. It is not a "contract," in the literal sense, which would be signed by all citizens or by their representatives and would define the common "values" of all French people and constitute the basis for the institutions of the Republic and relations between citizens. The republican pact as it "really exists" is produced by the totality of institutional, political and ideological state apparatuses that create "consent" (Gramsci), that "morally" bind those defined as citizens between themselves and to the state, that is to say, that it produces the identification of citizens with the dominant political order. The republican pact is therefore a construction of the state that has restarted many times through the crises and metamorphoses that have accompanied the state's gradual institutionalization and stabilization since the Revolution.

Scholars have often emphasized the democratic, social, and national aspects through which the state took form. Its racial aspect and the relation between this and other aspects have generally been overlooked.

Just as the Republic took a century to stabilize, the racial pact on which it relies would also take a century to become stable. It was the master stroke of the Third Republic. It institutionalized French nationalism, racialism, and colonialism as *inseparable* realities. We could, of course, identify the similar, incomplete, and confused forms which paved the way for this, but their systematization as *state policy* was clearly the (foundational) work of the Third Republic.

The historian Gérard Noiriel notes that in the 1880s the "defense of the homeland became a sacred theme"[32] both on the right and on the left of the political spectrum. But what "homeland" are we talking about? To begin, this point must be emphasized: the French nation is not the expression of a French "ethnicity" with roots extending deep into a thousand year history. Nor is it the spontaneous, "contractual" political gathering of a people that everything conspired to unite. The French nation, with the shape and content that we know, is a *republican institution*. It only exists through the state that caused it to exist as it itself came into existence. Under the Ancien Régime, the territory that is today associated with the French nation, as if this were self-evident, was far from unified. The very notion of a border was hazy and not systematic before the end of the eighteenth century. While the absolute monarchy began the work of political, legal, and administrative unification of a large part of the territories and the populations that form contemporary France, the Revolution and then the First Empire did the most to shape it. However, this work of unification was far from complete until the end of the nineteenth century.

In dominant media, political, and often academic discourse, the idea of the French nation is ambivalent to say the least. The nation is supposedly constituted by *those who want it* and *those who deserve it*. It is allegedly both "civic," proceeding from a foundational contract between free and equal citizens who form the political body as the source of popular sovereignty, *and*, whether expressed explicitly or implicitly, it is purportedly the expression of a national reality that is revealed to itself through a thousand-year history, the incarnation of a "French character" particular to an initially divided people that a specific destiny unified within "natural" borders. Whether the emphasis is placed on either one of these positions, and to the extent that they might seem opposed, in truth both facets of this explanation are intertwined. They are both complementary and contradictory. Ethnicity and civic character come face to face, but at the same time, ethnicity is already present at the heart of "civic" character. Or rather, the latter is constitutive of ethnicity in that, understood as the expression of "French character," it justifies French supremacy over other nations. The universal is supposedly immanent to the French nation, the "nation of human rights," whereas other nations are ostensibly particularistic. France would thus have the "destiny" or "mission" of leading the rest of humanity to the universal. Although national, the French nation would have a transnational vocation, in effect abolishing its own borders.[33] These contradictions, present since the Revolution, remain at the heart of the French conception of the nation.

Beyond the discourses on the nation, its concrete construction as ethnic nation was carried out primarily by the Third Republic.[34] This Republic emerged from a double trauma. First, the French defeat to Germany in 1870. Second, the Paris Commune, which was the first major defeat of the new dominant class. The Third Republic was therefore established both as a reaction to the dominant classes clustered around the bourgeoisie, and as a national reaction dissimulating this fact. The French nation, whose "identity" the current president claims to defend, is a political construction. It is the product of political relations of power crystalized in a state that had, in the end, appeared too fragile and incapable of containing, controlling, and integrating the popular classes. To avoid the return of the monarchy or of empire, to affirm its power in the face of other European powers, to get rid of the old dominant classes and infra or para-state allegiances (important local dignitaries, the church), and to avoid popular revolt, the Republic had to be supplemented by the nation. Either it gave itself a true empire or it died of its contradictions.

The nationalization of France was therefore a deliberate policy. The nation was constructed *from the top*, impelled by the Republic, which built many institutions meant to trace the boundaries of French society as a statutory grouping, to solidify feelings of belonging, norms, and other distinctions, to homogenize a heterogeneous people, and to replace the different mediations and agents of socialization that preexisted the state or contested its preeminence with centralized state bodies. The nation-state was instituted through centralization, through the administrative and police unification of the territory, and through surveillance and close control of the population. It came about by evicting, disqualifying, or subordinating local and regional dignitaries and by the promotion of new elites. It instituted compulsory military service. It outlawed or integrated into its institutional network any collective entity that could stand between the central power and the individual liable to develop intermediary "community effects," or to reinforce the competing identities of state ethnicity. It fought the para-state structure of the Catholic clergy (through laws on secularity) and religious ideology by attempting to replace it, for better or worse, with the sacralization of the national Republic. It generalized education under the auspices of cohorts of republican schoolteachers, carried out cultural and linguistic unification through authoritarian means, fought traditions, destroyed, reorganized, absorbed all traditional customs, and intervened on all the levels of the construction of social and individual life. It was necessary for the republican social bond to be transmitted through the state's own bodies and only through them. The nation-state produced and propagated the fantasy of a glorious and triumphant French history. It exalted one of the most chauvinistic nationalisms, obsessed by the ambition of "recovering" the Alsace-Lorraine region and reinvigorated by the "great feats of arms" of colonial troops.

The invention of the "right to nationality" played a major role in delimiting the nation. The notion of "nationality" as we understand it today is very recent in France and in the other European countries. It emerged both as a product of internal political stakes and within the framework of establishing international law that would regulate disputes between the great white powers and solidify their supremacy over a colonized world, or one that was being colonized. Conceptualized gradually, the "right to nationality" brought about the *contemporary* distinction between "nationals" and "foreigners," a distinction founded on increasingly unequal civil rights and the revocation of the principal attributes of citizenship. Nationality is therefore not a simple individual characteristic that reflects one's origin, birthplace or place of residence, or culture, but the legal-political codification of a particular social relation that the state constructs by relying on any of these individual characteristics. The national distinction that is naturalized and fetishized today did not hold sway under the Ancient Regime, which was based on the estate system and whose members were defined as "subjects" of the king. It remained vague and often contradictory in the immediate aftermath of the Revolution of 1789, which moved first to found the nation on citizenship and citizenship of residence (notwithstanding other restrictions linked to gender, social condition, etc.). The democratic impetus of the Revolution was rapidly quelled. It was mostly in the second half of the nineteenth century and more particularly under the Third Republic, however, that the contemporary sense of nationality was established, barring non-nationals from citizenship, deepening the gap in civil rights between French and non-French, and through multiple laws, decrees, administrative memorandums and other secret orders and policing measures that corseted entry, residency, work, and freedom of circulation in France. In sum, the Third Republic endeavored to regulate all of the dimensions of the social life of foreigners, at least those whose presence the Republic had tolerated on its territory, those whom it considered indispensable to the vitality of the mines and manufactures that French proletarians and peasants stayed away from, all of those it considered "easily assimilated," "loyal," culturally predisposed to integrating "Frenchness," joining the ranks of the grunts destined to die one day on a European front, or, for the luckiest of them, smoking out some uncooperative ragheads. When the notion of "nationality" was codified into law in 1889 for the first time, it was already saturated with culturalism, ethnicism, and racialism. The ardent xenophobia of the French population under the Third Republic should come as no surprise, no more than the antisemitic fervor that sent Dreyfus to Devil's Island before tarnishing France in the 1930s once again. We know the rest...

Rejecting all those who are considered foreigners from the nation does not simply establish a border between an inside and an outside. It also dissolves the border between citizenship and nationality, between the nation as body politic and ethnic nation. More than this, citizenship is absorbed into nationality; the nation is embodied in the state and in its border blockades, whereas the state is embodied in the ethnicized content of the nation. Henceforth, individuals are nationals no longer because they belong to a political body whose sovereignty develops through the state, but first because they "belong" to the national state. Nationality becomes the principal *content* of citizenship. As Etienne Balibar rightly states, "the great equivalence set up by modern states between *citizenship* and *nationality* (which actually provides the content for the idea of 'popular sovereignty') then begins to operate opposite to its democratic meaning: not in order to turn nationality into the historical figure of the construction collective freedom and equality, but to make it the very essence of citizenship, the absolute community that all other communities must reflect."[35] The Republic is only faced with individuals, but they are not atomized, or not only so. They are also nationalized individuals. They consider themselves to be free individuals, but they are in reality the property of the state.

You could say that I am describing a totalitarian society, that the aims of the Third Republic were only partially realized, stymied by the social and cultural weight of society, and that they ran up against divergent interests, struggles, and resistance. You could say that I forget to highlight the profusion of the freedoms granted or won, the flourishing of democratic forms, the development of the press, of unions, and of parties. You could claim that I did not mention universal (male) suffrage and the wealth of parliamentary life, that the generalization of education, the integration of the French people, the marginalization of the Church, and the definitive defeat of the monarchy expanded the field of citizenship. Admittedly, and yet we have known for a long time that democracy can also be totalitarian. But most of all, we know that from the Third Republic up to today the principal tools of democracy have been the exclusive, statutory privilege of French people and of white French people.

But let us continue...

Because the republican pact is not simply national. It is also social. Or, more exactly, it is national because it is social and social because it is national.

Just as political ties must henceforth occur in the immediate relation between each individual and the state, economic links are supposed to occur in the immediate relation between individuals who are free and equal in the face of the law. But social reality is nearsighted or hypocritical; it does not recognize juridical reality. Social conflicts do not oppose individuals but groups of individuals. And at all times, the clash of their antagonistic interests threatens to destroy "social cohesion," which is nothing other than "national cohesion." Against liberal doctrine, the state must then intervene at all levels of the social life of individuals (in education, training, health, living conditions, work, relations with employers...). It develops its own means to socialize, protect, and negotiate, that is, to integrate into the nation-state. Faced with the stubborn tendency of individuals to come together to defend their common interests, the state is forced to tolerate and then institutionalize a certain number of autonomous collective bodies such as parties and unions. Although it does not always succeed, it nonetheless persists in making sure that all the mechanisms that constitute the fields of politics and of citizenry function as instruments for national integration. The social state takes shape through *nationalized* citizenship. Although already very apparent in the nineteenth century, the nationalization of citizenship continued to intensify under the Third Republic, in particular through the establishment of a legal arsenal that sanctioned the inequality between "national" workers and foreigners in terms of social, civil, and political rights. "National preference" and the xenophobic national ideology that it produced therefore became constitutive elements of the social dimension of the republican pact. By fomenting rivalries between French and foreign workers that were always to the benefit of the former, the Republic cemented its national dimension even further. But just as French workers were privileged compared to foreign workers from other European states, these foreign workers were privileged compared to workers from the colonies. In the first case, national difference was involved, in the second, it was racial difference. The national social pact is also a *racial* pact.

National "Gallic" integration within the space of the French borders was juxtaposed with a national colonial integration around belonging to a statutory "French" group, itself within the context of the larger statutory grouping of white-European civilization. National identity, constructed both in relation to Europe and to colonized peoples, thus blended two types of partly antagonistic identities. The first was specifically *national*, shaped around the myth of an eternal France with supposedly Gallic origins. The second was *transnational*, created around a white-European-Christian supremacy of supposedly Greek origins whose first borders were the French territories of the empire. French national identity, which knits the republican pact together and flows through social logics and state politics, is an imperial identity, or, in other words, colonial/racial. The French nation is an *imperial nation.*

The nation-state was constructed in the same movement that led imperial expansion. Colonists were not only metropolitan populations that were exported and reproduced in the colonies. They were also white metropolitan populations whose many rights and privileges were immediately linked to the global indigenous relation. There is no need to recall here the statutory hierarchies established by colonization since slavery, then with the different "indigenal" versions, of which the indigenous system in Algeria was perhaps the most developed. The right to nationality, and the notions of assimilation and then of integration are perhaps the most manifest expressions of the presence of race in the nation. The multitude of discrimination that has affected and continues to affect the populations coming from the colonies does not simply attest to the importing of race relations that developed outside of France. They show that these race relations were already present and ready to receive the colonized in metropolitan France, populations that carried the colonial relation within themselves, in their bodies and in their histories. The French nation, as an imperial nation, was thus constituted as the interweaving of national and white groups, reserving complete citizenship and nationality for those who were considered fully human—or fully civilized, which is the same thing—in other words, whites. Whiteness is a dimension of national identity, an ideological substrate of the republican pact.

It bears repeating that the colonies were not outside of France. "The colony as such," notes Françoise Vergès, "is constitutive of the French nation. It is neither an excess nor its unreasonable elsewhere. The colonial has too often been understood as the exception when in fact it models the very body of the Republic."[36] In the same vein, Balibar writes that "all modern 'nations' are a product of colonization. They have always been colonizer or colonized to some extent, and sometimes both."[37] The constitution of the French nation was not an exclusively internal process. Just like other nations, it was constituted within the framework of the competitive partition of the world. The colonial state is constantly overflowing the official limits of its sovereignty, jostling its limits, and blending with other spaces of power to remodel or absorb them, or to impose on them the authority of its specific institutions. It insinuates itself, spreads, and digs its own canals through the powers that it either colonizes or covets. Therefore, "French society" is not *only* French. It is not restricted to the French metropolitan territory and to its populations, as the fetishistic illusion of borders would have us believe. "French society" is the movement that spreads in concentric circles from its state center—the core and apex of the French/white group—to engulf the other human communities that it subordinates to the colonial logic. The closer you are to the first circle, the more privileges and powers you have. "French society" is therefore constituted by the totality of social, political, and cultural mediations, and by the procedures, apparatuses, institutions, and abstract logics that only enable the white bourgeois to exist because the indigenous from Martinique, Senegal, Vietnam or Tunisia exist on the other end of the chain. "French society" is a colonial mechanism. It is the temporal and spatial continuum through which the colonial relation is permanently reconstituted, ruptured, and reshaped in racial confrontations and power relations. It is a closed space, saturated with borders, and it is also an open space without barriers that spreads, weaves in and out, snakes through, pierces, and soaks into other human societies to sustain the bulwark of white privilege. "French society" is fluid, a white liquid that soaks into the indigenous sponge. It is a solvent that annihilates indigenous resistance, a liquid that hardens into a truncheon smashing an indigenous skull or into the rope that hung Larbi Ben Mhidi. "French society" is white supremacy.

I am getting carried away. Forget all of this. What I want to emphasize is that French society is not circumscribed by its metropolitan borders. Although its institutions and its political relations of power are national, they are also integrated in an international arena. The same applies to colonial time, which is an unstable mixture of the contemporaneous and the non-contemporaneous, an unsteady amalgamation of local, "French," and global temporalities. It is not anachronistic to speak of colonialism today. Colonialism and postcolonialism are constantly groping each other under the table. Despite the victories of the wars of independence, the national republican pact today remains a racial pact. Whiteness continues to be at the center of the French nation while indigenous distinctions no longer differentiate specific territorial entities but have also penetrated the mainland itself. The relation of identity on which the republican pact is formed—and which gave its purpose to the Ministry of Immigration under Brice Hortefeux between 2007–2009—can be expressed in two statements: 1. French people are white; 2. The best whites are French.

3

Why We Should Hate Charles de Gaulle

> "*The great victory of the Vietnamese people at Dien
> Bien Phu is no longer strictly speaking a Vietnamese
> victory. [...] The colonial governments are therefore
> gripped in a genuine wholesale panic. Their plan is
> to make the first move, to turn the liberation move-
> ment to the right and disarm the people: Quick, let's
> decolonize. [...] In answer to the strategy of a Dien
> Bien Phu defined by the colonized, the colonizer
> replies with the strategy of containment—respecting
> the sovereignty of nations.*"
>
> —Frantz Fanon, *The Wretched of the Earth*

De Gaulle was not the hero of decolonization
but the *French strategist of the colonial counter-
revolution*. His role (and his ambition) while in
power was to try to resolve the crisis of the
national-republican pact. We must start from
this point.

De Gaulle was first and foremost a French *nationalist*. He was a statesman in the strong sense of the term inasmuch as his own thinking not only merged with "state thinking," but as a military man, he was a man of the central institution of the state, the army, a professional corps whose role is to defend the state and the nation, and more precisely to uphold the form of their intimate connection, the nation-state. Or, in other words, its role is to defend the statutory hierarchies on which the state and the nation/empire are based. We could say that the vocation of the military corps embodied by de Gaulle is simply to defend *borders*. But we should immediately clarify that all borders are *statutory* borders, as defined previously. The army defends the borders internal to the *white world* (in relation to other European states or to the United States) that we could call national, borders that are internal *to France*, in particular racial ones, and the borders between *whites and indigenous* throughout this world. These priorities can at times be complementary or conflated, and sometimes antagonistic. The French army's capitulation in 1940 to the external-internal enemy, an enemy external to France and internal to the white world, was a terrible dilemma. So was the French army's defeat by revolts led by the peoples of the empire, that is to say by the internal-external enemy, an enemy internal to French political space and external to the white world. De Gaulle's self-appointed "mission" was to resolve this dilemma.

For this reason, de Gaulle took power on two occasions. The first was self-proclaimed, when the national republic was threatened by German occupation. The second occurred through a coup d'état, when the national-racial republic was threatened by anti-colonial revolution. In other words, de Gaulle took power to avoid the total collapse of the republican pact. He presented himself first as the representative of "Free France" against the Vichy Regime. His goal, as presented in the program of the National Council of the Resistance, was to "reestablish France in its power, its grandeur, and its universal mission." After the Liberation, the national union that was established around the general patched up the republican pact to the best of its abilities. Yet the crisis was far from over because the United States, which had already benefitted from the first inter-European conflict, was definitively taking the place of the European powers. France, like Great Britain, had become secondary powers. At the Yalta conference that partitioned the world between the United States and the USSR, France was unceremoniously pushed aside. The national republic had a hard time absorbing the shock. However, it still hoped—and this was de Gaulle's role—to recover its place among the greatest nations, especially by relying on its colonial empire. It was a misjudgment of the new state of power relations. The Second World War had greatly weakened both nation-states and colonial empires. In the aftermath of liberation, France faced with subduing protest movements and revolutions brewing in its colonies: with the Sétif and Guelma massacres on May 8, 1945 (the day of the French Liberation!), the deadly bombing of Haiphong in North Vietnam, and killings in Madagascar... But neither the most barbarian repression, nor institutional reform (such as the constitution of 1946 that instituted the French Union and laws giving some semblance of citizenship to the indigenous), nor de Gaulle and his successors could stop the wave of anti-colonial conflicts that disintegrated the empire. At Dien Bien Phu in May 1945, colonial troops suffered a massive beating. The Algerian National Liberation Front (FLN) began its insurrection a few months later. Both the United States and the USSR encouraged decolonization more or less directly and strengthened their influence in the colonies. The death knell of the colonial empire had sounded. France gave up its territories one by one. In 1958, when General de Gaulle returned to the presidential palace, carried by the revolt of the Pieds-Noirs and the strong-arm tactics of the French Algerian army, the empire was already falling apart. *The empire, or in other words, the Republic.*

Historians disagree as to whether de Gaulle still favored a French Algeria at the time or if he was already convinced that France had no other choice but to let go of its Algerian "departments."[38] What seems certain, however, is that he only consented to the loss of the colonies because he was forced into it. Indeed, he did all he could to keep them as long as he felt it could be done without contributing to the internal dislocation of the French state. It seems that he hesitated over which strategy to follow in Algeria. It was not to keep the colonial form intact, which was the motivation of the military generals behind the Algerian putsch that had brought him to power. Instead, his hesitation was over the *possible* way to preserve French supremacy given the new reality of power relations. He therefore consistently acted to weaken the power of the national Algerian movement, temporize, and unify his own camp. The cautious retreat he initiated, which was purely tactical, became a strategic retreat in light of the circumstances—or more precisely due to the power of the Algerian will— leading to the inevitable, that is to say the Evian Accords (1962). Socialist leader Guy Mollet recounts how de Gaulle explained the strategy he would follow during a meeting on May 30, 1958. He meant to provoke the division of Algeria into different communities (Kabyle, Arab, Berber, European, Jewish), each with a certain autonomy in the framework of a "federal solution" organized under French leadership "such that a majority could never impose its will on a minority in any of the communities."[39] Responding to Vincent Auriol on the same day, when he described the dangers of the "integration" desired by the French military in Algeria and especially the risk of having one hundred and twenty-five Algerian delegates in the National Assembly and as many for Sub-Saharan Africa, de Gaulle clarified "I am in favor of the federative system, for the African, Algerian federations, crowned by a confederation with France, which will be a confederation of associated peoples."[40] The general therefore contemplated dividing French Africa into "communities" (often made up by the French!) federated among themselves and assembled in a French-led confederation. Already present in the first proposition for a constitution laid out by de Gaulle, the project quickly evolved under pressure from African separatists to become a confederation of autonomous states—or more precisely, vassal administrations of the French state—that would continue to hold effective sovereignty through its executive branch and, more precisely, the president of the Republic.[41] This confederation, which was labeled an "association" for a time, would become the French Community. This colonial reorganization would be institutionalized by the new constitution—

and this fact is too often forgotten—that was not only a national constitution but also an imperial one. Nonetheless, it did give the possibility of voting "no" on the constitutional referendum of October 4, 1958 to those peoples who refused it on principle. In the same way, each state was granted the right to leave the French Community and to recover its sovereignty at will. Community institutions were set up in 1959, integrating all the French colonies of Sub-Saharan Africa, with the notable exception of Guinea, whose nationalist leader Sékou Touré had called for the refusal of the constitution. Still, this new colonial architecture would not survive the rise of nationalism for very long. De Gaulle quickly back-pedaled and looked to other options to preserve French domination over Sub-Saharan Africa and prevent the radicalization of anti-colonial movements. In December 1959, he thus opened the way for the "international sovereignty" of the Sub-Saharan states. The constitutional law of June 4, 1960 instituted a contractual community ruled by bi- or multilateral accords between France and the new states.[42] By 1963, the case was closed, and yet de Gaulle's colonial determination remained unchanged. "*Françafrique*" was up and running, financially bonded to the French metropole by the CFA franc. It would be the role of Jacques Foccart—the general's henchman at the head of the African network of the Rally of the

French People[43] since 1947, the orchestrator of the coup attempt in Algiers on May 13, 1958, ex-secretary general of the Community, secretary for African and Madagascan Affairs—to build the new imperial form for Sub-Saharan Africa. A set of (political, military, financial, cultural) cooperation agreements organizing the new independent states' allegiance to France would replace the relations of domination institutionalized within the frame-work of the Community. Foccart placed puppets as heads of state. He arranged to eliminate—often violently—the nationalist leaders who refused to submit to France, and even some more moderate ones who were unwilling to forego all dignity.[44] He stirred up rivalries and conflicts, and provoked "ethnic" seditions. In sum, he used any means necessary to bolster France's authority over what has been called its "African turf," the last bastion of its international influence.

De Gaulle's rise to power was the result of the *political relations of power* constructed in the opposition between colonial and indigenous power. The historical conditions that propelled the general to the pinnacle of state power were not determined primarily by the "congenital flaws" of the parliamentary system, nor directly by class struggle, but by the political powerlessness of the colonial state faced with the assaults of the Algerian revolution in a global context where France had lost much of its international reserves of power, and where the Algerian people had, on their end, won reserves of power from the struggles of other indigenous peoples against domination. The political crisis in France that de Gaulle used to his advantage was a refraction of the struggle of social races on a global scale. The crisis of the colonial republic—which was not simply the crisis of the Fourth Republic—was the crisis of white domination; in other words, it was the crisis of the racial dimension of the republican pact.

Algerian anti-colonial power could not win through its military might alone, due to the enormous technological, logistic, and economic differences with France. It could only win politically. That is to say, it could only be victorious through the political effects of the war in France. The principal expression of these political effects was an eruption of contradictions: 1. at the heart of the political leadership of the colonial state (in the executive branch, the parliament, and the party system); 2. at the heart of its military leadership; 3. between the political and military leadership; 4. between metropolitan France (state, society ...) and French colonial society (local political, administrative, and military bodies, populations of colonists). What characterized the situation before the events of May 13, 1958 was therefore the "powerlessness of the different spheres" of colonial power. None was truly able to resolve the crisis for its own ends, whereas Algerian nationalism, powerless for its part to win in strictly military terms, already possessed political power potentially superior to that of the colonial state. When de Gaulle took hold of the reins of state power, the relations of power were in unstable equilibrium. To paraphrase a famous author, I am tempted to say that the colonizers could *no longer* impose colonization, and that the colonized could *not yet* impose independence. De Gaulle had no other choice but to prioritize resolving the internal political crisis. On their end, the Algerians, despite their own crises, continued to insist on their principal demand: political independence. The balance of power was increasingly shifting in their favor: independence was becoming possible. It was won in 1962, with a few concessions. For all that, the reality of global political relations of power would not enable the Algerian people—or any other peoples engaged in struggle—to emancipate themselves from all colonial oversight.

We would of course need to dissect the mediations through which these global relations of power reverberated at the heart of Algerian nationalism, and to evoke the endogenous logics and the internal conflicts of an Algerian society reconfigured by one hundred and thirty years of colonial oppression. But that is not my purpose here. However, I will say more about the relations of power internal to the French political field in order to emphasize the decisive nature of the colonialist/anti-colonialist divide. The splintering of political currents under the Fourth Republic and their tactical differences in regard to the "Algerian problem" did not, in fact, preclude a broad consensus on the need to preserve French predominance in Algeria. Even the French Communist Party, whose parliamentary representatives voted to grant "emergency powers" to the Socialist Guy Mollet in 1956,[45] was satisfied with a demand for "peace." Communist militants would nonetheless individually join the anti-colonial struggle alongside left-wing Christian movements, Trotskyists, and anarchists. While in May 1958, centrists and Socialists attempted to block de Gaulle's ascent as propelled by the military general staff, their stance was less in relation to the Algerian question than because they feared being removed from power themselves. Under these conditions and given his talent for playing off antagonisms and fears, de Gaulle stood a good chance of winning. And on June 2, 1958, the National Assembly relinquished power in his favor. For more than ten years, the "man of June 18" would embody France, or more specifically the spirit of the reigning bureaucratic "caste." If we were to express his politics in an extremely concise way, we could say they endeavored to consolidate the national state against social, political, and institutional factors of internal disintegration and to consolidate its global power against other white states. His colonial strategy came from the same perspective, as did his "class" politics. His aims were the same as at the Liberation of France in 1940.

The Fifth Republic was therefore not simply a constitutional formula to overcome the parliamentary bedlam characteristic of the previous republic. It was the product of the political relations of power determined by the crisis of the national and colonial pact that led to its creation.[46] It was an attempt to resolve the crisis of the national Republic. Granting so many powers to the executive branch and to its leader was not a simple technical solution imposed by a military man following authoritarian traditions, but a way to free the state and its bureaucracy from party supervision and from the harmful effect of class struggle on national unity. It was a means to solidify the bureaucratic pyramid under the yoke of a supreme leader who would personify the nation and be capable of realizing the old republican dream, the standardization and rallying of all "French people" around the state. The second component of de Gaulle's strategy to resolve the national crisis was to restore the power of the French state within the global interstate system. De Gaulle understood the future of the colonial empire from that perspective, as a resource for power, leverage in the competition opposing France to the other "great nations," and the very symbol of French magnificence. But once the imperial glory began to fade, once the colonies became a source of crises, provoking discord, breaking institutions apart, and draining the national energy, then it was time to abandon the empire, or at least to give up on the direct administration of its dominated peoples. In addition, national military power no longer lay in the pounds of flesh that could be aligned on the battlefield. As a gigantic reserve of military manpower, the empire was obsolete. It was the time of nuclear deterrence, which was the central aim of General de Gaulle's defense strategy, complementing efforts to reinforce French technological potential, particularly in information technology. The other components of the Gaullist strategy stemmed from the same ambition. When he attempted to reinforce the French economy under the auspices of the state and to protect businesses from foreign competition, when he refused the supremacy of the dollar, or when he tried to institute paternalistic relations between the employer class and the working class, de Gaulle's intent was always to overcome the national crisis, that is to say to consolidate the economic and institutional foundations of the state, to dissipate internal tensions, and to restore "France's place in the world."

This was of course the aim of his international policies. There could be no "great nation," thought the general, without a great international policy. In the "concert of nations," a nice euphemism evoking the hierarchical global interstate structure, he had to be on his toes. Split in two by the Berlin wall and shaken by the global third estate, the system of states had become an unstable assemblage. White supremacy was no longer what it once had been. Its center had definitively shifted from "old Europe" to its former American colony. Moscow? Moscow was perhaps a second center, but Moscow was not completely white. The Soviet capital was the *moujik* capital, just barely out of the Middle Ages, and it was the heart of the power of the "dangerous classes." Most importantly, however, the Soviet Union was not Europe. It was the Europe of the Slavs, who, as suggests, were former slaves. They were also strangely Christian, and not really white. Moscow was Eastern Europe. The Orient, to be frank. The barbarian and Muslim Asia that was jeopardizing the *real* Europe. Between the two world wars, the Bolshevik revolution had already been explicitly condemned as a threat to white civilization.[47] Asian hordes descending on Europe, Judeo-Bolshevik plots, European anti-communism always served to defend white supremacy (even when the "dictatorship *over* the proletariat" proved itself to be a dictatorship of the non-white peoples of the Soviet Empire). According to Jean-Raymond Tournoux, a Pétainist journalist who converted to Gaullism, the general asserted that "Russian communists are traitors to the white race. One day they shall once again be united with Europe."[48]

De Gaulle never betrayed his camp. It was out of the question that France would abandon its defense of the West. Au contraire! In his eyes, France was the bastion of the white world. And even though the unfortunate circumstances of history seemed to have momentarily decided otherwise, in the end it would return to its destiny. At least as long as it adopted a leader like Him. A leader who would know how to pull the strings of history. Concretely, it meant someone who would remain friends with its friends while extending a hand to its friends' enemies. Between 1958 and 1961, he endeavored to have NATO, the military instrument of white domination, serve as the framework for an equal partnership between the United States, Great Britain, and France. The United States refused, just as they refused to help France acquire nuclear weapons. From then on, de Gaulle no longer hesitated. Despite his support for the United States during the Cuban missile crisis, he left NATO. In the new context of détente, with some leeway in relation to his own camp in the white world, he tried in vain to lead Germany toward building a Europe under French leadership. He also defended a number of positions and initiatives that ran counter to American policies: recognizing communist China in 1964, criticizing American policy in Indochina, condemning Israel in October 1967, travelling to the USSR, and attempting to get a foothold in Latin America, among others. France, whose ascendancy over part of Africa had not (yet) been contested by the United States, was trying to reestablish the international foundations of its power.

The illusion was short lived, in this case and for other matters. The crisis of the white national republic, inaugurated by the collapse of the empire, therefore remained partly unresolved. The events of May-June 1968 must be reframed in the context of that crisis. It is of course quite strange (but oh! how meaningful) that it is always considered a global youth uprising, a generational crisis, a class struggle ("the ten thousand strikers"), a leftist-libertarian outburst, an abrupt transition into "modernity," or the emergence of "societal" conflicts but not as the product of the huge event that came *immediately* before, that is, anti-colonial revolution. I would insist on the term "immediately." Why is this temporal proximity never mentioned? Why do we fail to understand the political crisis that finally led to the expulsion of General de

Gaulle as the indirect result of anti-colonial revolution and the effect of the divisions that it produced in French political space? Historians sometimes mention that the "ideals" (or alternatively, the "illusions") of Third-Worldism strongly permeated the rebellious youth. But that is as far as it goes. In her analysis of the causes of May 1968, Kirstin Ross[49] is one of the rare scholars to have highlighted the decisive influence of the Algerian Revolution and the Vietnam War on the 1968 protesters.[50] She does, however, note that the colonialist positions of the leadership of the French Communist Party spurred a significant portion of the youth to leave institutional communism in favor of far left movements that gave more credence to the colonial question. More importantly, indigenous power continued to act in an almost underground manner through the political processes at the heart of the old metropolis. Such an extensive regime crisis concurrent with a huge social protest movement can only be explained by an upheaval of the state—and more generally of French society—for which the fundamental cause was decolonization. Of course, I am not trying to mask the other causes of May 68, but we would be missing one of its essential components if we did not also see it as a *delayed effect of the anti-colonial revolution* that undermined some of the fundamental principles of the republican pact. From that point of view, May

68 appeared as the first major expression of the failure of the general's great project of national integration which was meant to replace the imperial nation.

Colossal by the scope of the popular mobilization it provoked, the revolt in 1968 also revealed redeployments and new divisions at the heart of the Right and in the high spheres of the state apparatus. The prodigious victory of the "party of law and order" in the legislative elections of June 1968 only provided the general with a brief respite. He was contested at the heart of his own camp by George Pompidou who had long been his loyal prime minister. And still on the right, the movement led by Valéry Giscard d'Estaing was impatient to break down the Gaullist hegemony. The "man of June 18," who should more appropriately be called the "man of May 13, 1958," rose up and attempted a final maneuver to free himself from "his" right, and then fell. That was the referendum, or rather, the ultimatum of 1969. De Gaulle had announced he would leave power if he lost. That decision tipped the balance: a majority of French people answered "no" and ushered him into retirement in Colombey.

I will not insist on the redeployments and ruptures within the ranks of the Right in the decade that followed, or on the intensity of social protest that enabled the Left to win the 1981 elections, thus shifting the political axis of white power for a while. In the following pages, I will concentrate on the appearance and metamorphoses of a new indigenous power at the very heart of the French political field. De Gaulle considered France a white nation protected from the repercussions of the struggles of dominated peoples. It was not the least of his failures: the anti-colonial struggles moved into the very heart of France, and France is no longer white.

4

First Racial Skirmishes in the Heart of France

"[...] the French still live with their superiority,
except that it's buried more deeply inside them,
lower down, probably in the depths of their intes-
tines. This once haughty superiority, aware that its
days are numbered, is growing vicious. And it's all
the more irritated now that France is full of blacks,
Arabs, people of mixed race who almost never lower
their eyes anymore: their gaze is on a level with ours."
—Jean Genet, 1979[51]

"When the bombs fell on Hanoi, we had a few epi-
dermal reactions. During the Korean War too. The
killing was happening far away. Here and now, we
can see that our colonized people, who perhaps still
appear to us like shadows in our midst, are about to
become our adversaries in our own country."
—Jean Genet, 1979[52]

Yes, de Gaulle did not consider France to be anything other than a white nation! "'We need more than just fine words!' he admitted. 'It's all fine and good for there to be yellow, black, and brown French people. They show that France is open to all races and prove its universal mission. But it is on the condition that they remain a small minority. Otherwise, France would no longer be France. We are a European people, a white race, with a Greek and Latin culture, and with a Christian religion. Don't let them lie to us! Have you seen Muslims? Have you looked at them up close, with their turbans and their djellabas? It's clear they're not French! […] Try to mix oil and vinegar. Shake the bottle. After a while, they will separate. Arabs are Arabs; the French are French. Do you think that the French social body can absorb ten million Muslims, who will be twenty million tomorrow, and forty million the day after? If we follow through with integration, if all the Arabs and Berbers of Algeria were considered French, how could we stop them from coming to live in the metropolitan France where the standard of living is so much higher? My village would no longer be called Colombey-les-Deux-Eglises (Colombey-The-Two-Churches) but Colombey-les-Deux-Mosquées (Colombey-The-Two-Mosques)!'"[53] Or: "You know, I've had enough of your negroes. You are taking liberties. They are everywhere.

There are negroes at the Elysée Palace every day, you ask me to see them, you have me take them to lunch. I'm surrounded by negroes here. [...] And it's completely pointless! I won't be bothered with your negroes! I don't want to see any for two months, you understand? No more interviews with any negroes for two months. It's not really because of how much time it takes, even if it is really a hassle, but it projects a very bad image: all you see are negroes, every day, at the Elysée Palace. And let me tell you, it's absolutely pointless."[54]

I could quote endlessly from his works, and from the declarations and provisions drafted during his tenure. They would all testify to the fact that in addition to his nationalist arrogance, de Gaulle was also a white supremacist. I will just mention the nomination of Georges Mauco to head the Haut Comité Consultatif de la Population et de la Famille (Consultative Committee on Population and the Family) created in April 1945. Mauco was a noteworthy proponent of racism and antisemitism in the 1930, and one of the most influential personalities in his chosen area under the Vichy regime. The sociologist Alexis Spire, a specialist on the subject, notes that, at the end of the war, "a third, even half"[55] of the institution that Mauco directed was comprised of officials who had spearheaded the Vichy family policies. He adds that "the senior officials who were promoted to positions in the Ministry of Population at the Liberation belonged in large part to a Christian-Democratic vein open to immigration from Europe but hostile to the permanent settling of 'Muslim Algerian French' who were considered impossible to integrate."[56] Barely a month after the committee was created, de Gaulle presided over a meeting that established a "general directive" concerning the selection of immigrants "according to a hierarchy of determined 'desirability.'"[57] On June 12, 1945, Georges Mauco, also wishing to influence naturalization policies, sent a note to the general who would then repeat it almost word for word in a directive addressed to the Minister of Justice. This letter would merit reproduction in full as it illustrates both the racist demons of the man who inspired it, and the skill with which the republic could camouflage the inequalities it established. I will simply reproduce the first point here. It explicitly highlights the need, "in terms of *ethnicity*, to limit the influx of Mediterraneans and Orientals who have profoundly modified the human structure of France over the last half-century."[58] This directive would be considerably modified (and euphemized in its form) by the Interministerial Commission on Naturalization that rejected some of the discrimination under consideration but nonetheless emphasized that a "classification by nationality of origin of candidates would provide additional criteria" for naturalization. According to the minutes of a meeting of the naturalization committee cited by Patrick Weil, these criteria would only be relayed to "decision makers."[59]

There were of course other issues (such as the need for labor) that served to counteract this intended racial selection. And yet, although it has not always been the main priority, preserving the whiteness of the French nation has since remained a constant concern for public policy. In the 1960s, the main issue was importing a labor force. Although Southern European workers were favored, the government did not reject workers from the former colonies, negotiating with the newly independent states to purchase their muscle power in the best interests of France. It was thought at the time that these workers were not destined to settle in France. If they ever had that intention, everything was done to eliminate their desire to put down lasting roots.[60] The authorities notably attempted to limit the influx of Algerians, whose emigration to France had been facilitated by the Evian Accords. They tried to discourage family immigration, first of Algerians, then of all indigenous. "The derogatory status to which Algerians were often subjected," writes Alexis Spire, "also offered the French administration the opportunity to introduce a two-tiered family immigration system: one encouraging foreigners from the

European continent and the other dissuading those from the previously colonized countries."[61] The racial selection was obvious.

As one might suspect, everything was put in place to make immigrant workers malleable, docile, and exploitable at will, as well as to curtail any form of resistance and organization. Workers coming from the ex-colonies were spatially, socially, and culturally confined to the outskirts of French society. They were also supervised, controlled, and surveilled via a multiplicity of administrative, law enforcement, and social apparatuses that were often set up by civil servants who had gained direct experience in the colonies and who were transmitting this "colonial *savoir faire*" to their colleagues and successors. In the last years of the Gaullist regime, measures to restrict, select, and control immigration were reinforced against the advice of employers, who were recruiting foreign workers hand-over-fist to feed the "boom" of mass production and the growing automobile industry. However, the anti-indigenous offensive began to take on a more defined shape after the resignation of General de Gaulle. And since then, outside a few temporary ceasefires, it has continued to grow.

Immigration policies in the 1970s did not break with the strategic choices of the Republic. However, they took on new shapes and intensities determined by the internal stakes of the white political field as well as by the emergence of an indigenous political power that was deeply novel in its dynamic and its content. Following the Liberation, the social power of immigrants hailing from the colonies, and Algerians in particular, was considerably strengthened in concert with the reconstruction of war-torn France. In *political* terms, this *social* power appeared primarily in the anti-colonial struggle waged in the heart of metropolitan France. Until independence was achieved, the political power of immigrants could not be dissociated from the political power of the indigenous in the colonies. It represented one moment within the empire as a whole. When the empire collapsed, the unity of this process also fell apart. The space that had structured the lives of immigrants and given meaning to their political action was dismantled. Indigenous power in France fell back on itself! After the end of the Gaullist decade, the new immigrant struggles were aligned in a new configuration. They gained new meaning depending on the place assigned to immigrants in the framework of a solidifying neocolonial domination. From then on, immigrant resistances found meaning in the concatenation of two fields of conflict: in the relations between France and its ancient colonies, and in the racial struggles within France itself.

People have often said that immigrants kept a low profile, and it is probably true. Yet most of them did not give up on themselves. It could be called internal marronage. They held onto their identity. They preferred to stay amongst themselves. And they dreamt of return. It was already a form of resistance, and it remains so. Anti-colonialist resistance. There were not many other choices. "You slice your world into manageable segments. You segregate yourself within the safety zones white people haven't littered with barricades and land mines."[62] They were crushed by the weight of the colonial/postcolonial state, stuck in exhausting labor, and surrounded on all sides by a hostile society. They faced numerous bans targeting immigrants (freedom of association, etc.), as well as divisions by nationality or even by regional community. They frequently misunderstood the mechanisms, codes, and norms of social and political action in France, and were closely watched and surveilled by the institutions of their home countries. What else could they do but learn the "science of stealth" and cling to their dignity?[63] Besides, they considered their immigration to be temporary. It would have been demeaning to consider staying in the country that had destroyed their own as anything other than a last resort. And if, at times, they were ashamed of begging France for work, if all they asked was to be able to make a living in peace and to be treated with respect, and if they did not consider the meager amounts sent to relatives back home to be an advance on the vast reparations France owed its old colonies, it was simply because their modesty was just the visible face of the pride that had returned to them with the conquest of independence.

And yet, forms of resistance that transgressed prohibitions and overcame obstacles did exist. They were more readable, more visible because they made demands and were more organized. Mediated by class struggles, and often relayed by white labor unions and solidarity movements, a few of these struggles left traces, although their breadth and diversity were often underestimated, especially in the 1970s. And since immigrant workers have been seen as victims and nothing else, "scapegoats" without real political weight, the deep impact of their struggles has been overlooked. *The way their actions reshaped the political field has gone unnoticed.*

Without claiming to be exhaustive, a list of a few of these indigenous struggles is helpful in highlighting their importance. I would have done it in an appendix, if anyone read them…

In factories. *Mai 1968*: specialized workers at Renault-Billancourt organize a powerful strike. Immigrant workers of different nationalities out-line a preliminary form of self-organization.

January 1971: Moroccan, Algerian, Tunisian, Malian, and Senegalese workers strike at the Pennaroya factory (Saint-Denis). That same month, specialized workers mobilize at the Renault-Île Seguin factory in the Hauts-de-Seine near Paris. *May 1971*: specialized workers at Renault-Le Mans go on strike and occupy the factory. *May–June 1971*: Caribbean workers in the Alstrom factories lead an eleven-week strike. *August 1971*: workers from La Réunion mobilize at Simca-Chrysler (Poissy). *August–September–October 1971*: workers from North Africa and La Réunion lead a struggle in the Brandt factories, Lyon. *December 1971*: immigrant workers at the Pennaroya factories in Saint-Denis, Lyon and Escaudœuvres in northern France mobilize, followed by a long strike the next year. *April 1972*: In Fos-sur-Mer, the steel factory Davum is the site of a powerful immigrant mobilization that lasts several months. *May–June 1972*: very long immigrant-worker strike at the naval construction site of La Ciotat. *1975*: specialized workers strike at Renault-Billancourt. *December 1972*: Parisian garbage collectors strike. *January 1973*: workers at the steel company Somafer in the Moselle go on strike so that hiring conditions are respected. *March 1973*: 400 specialized workers strike at Renault-Billancourt. *May 1973*: immigrant workers strike at the Margoline factory in Gennevilliers and in

Nanterre in the Hauts-de-Seine. *February 1974*: Mauritian workers strike in Troyes (Aube). In Laval (Mayenne), Turkish and Pakistani workers strike for more than three weeks. *January 1975*: Mauritian workers, victims of trafficking benefiting the Foreign Legion, as well as Moroccans and Tunisians begin a hunger strike. Their movement resumes in March. *May–June 1975*: Strike at the Chausson factories in Gennevilliers. *March 1976*: strike with a four-week occupation of the Peugeot cycle factory in Sochaux (Doubs). *February 1977*: in Gravelines (Nord), immigrant workers strike on the construction site of the nuclear power plant. *March 1977*: specialized worker strike at the Eaton-Manil company in the Ardennes. *April 1978*: Algerian workers strike at the Déhé company. *June 1978*: 500 specialized workers, mostly Mauritian and Senegalese, go on strike at the press shop of Renault-Billancourt.

Housing-related issues. *1969*: rent strike by African workers in Ivry and Saint-Denis. *January 1970*: intense mobilization following the death by asphyxiation of five Africans in an immigrant housing center. *February 1970*: resistance against the destruction of the Massy slums and forced relocation. 459 Algerians and Tunisians refuse to move to the Sonacotra housing centers in Massy and Sainte-Geneviève-des-Bois. A few hundred people living in the "Portuguese slums" also refuse to be relocated to housing centers in Grigny (Essonne) when they had been promised rent-controlled public apartments (HLM). This movement would continue until 1973. *February 1971*: the prefect of Seine-Saint-Denis expresses his concern about the increase in rent strikes. From then on, protest movements in housing centers would become constant and grow on a massive scale after 1974–1975. In 1978, rents go unpaid in nearly fifty percent of housing centers. The rent strike by residents of Sonacotra (as many as 20,000 strikers in all of France) would continue from 1975 to 1980. *May–June 1971*: for a few weeks, Antillean workers occupy the Del Campo housing center in the Twelfth arrondissement in Paris. A similar action would later take place at the Astrid hotel. *December 1971*: In Montbéliard, 120 Algerian residents threatened with eviction from their housing center mobilize. That same year there would be countless rent strikes led by Sub-Saharan Africans against slumlords in Paris, Ivry, Pierrefitte, and Bondy.

Struggles for papers and against evictions. *September 1971*: mobilization against the deportation of Lauretta Fonseca, a young Portuguese woman known for her active support of immigrants in the Massy slums. *October 1971*: In Amiens, struggle against the deportation of Sadok Djeridi. *March 1972*: In Aix-en-Provence and Oyonnax, general strike of immigrant workers against deportations and for decent housing. In 1972, there are a large number of hunger strikes all over France. The movement grows the following year and spreads to most major French cities. *May 1972*: strike for residence and work permits. The construction sites of the EGCC company in Amiens and Sainte-Geneviève-de-Bois are paralyzed by a five-week strike. *October 1972*: fight against the deportation of Saïd Bouziri (leader of the Mouvement des travailleurs arabes or MTA) and Faouzia Bouziri that leads to the creation of the Comité de defense de la vie et des droits des travailleurs immigrés (CDVDTI, Committee for the Defense of the Life and Rights of Immigrant Workers). *December 1972*: In La Ciotat, a hunger strike led by four Tunisians demanding work permits; in Valence, after a police raid on a hotel, eighteen undocumented Tunisian workers are threatened with deportation. Two of them start a hunger strike. Three French citizens, including a chaplain, join them. On December 23, 1500 people march in the city while the priests of various parishes decide to eliminate midnight mass. *February 1973*: thirteen Tunisian workers occupy the Javel factory in Paris. They demand work permits. *March 1973*: protest in Belleville (Paris) by several thousand immigrant workers for the repeal of the Marcellin-Fontanet circulars and for work permits. *June 1973*: protest by undocumented people in Paris. A few days later, same scenario in Grasse (Alpes-Maritimes).

1973: protests against the deportation of Mohamed Laribi of the MTA, Mohamed Najeh, General Secretary of the CDVDTI, the pro-Palestinian Syrian militant Maurice Courbage, and the Maoist Algerian worker Larbi Boudjenana. *February 1974*: forty Moroccan farm workers start a strike in Aix-en-Provence to obtain work permits and for decent lodgings. *May 1974*: Turkish, Tunisian, and Moroccan workers occupy the ANPE (National Employment Agency) in Marseille. In the same month, a hundred Maghrebin and Pakistani immigrants occupy the departmental office for work and employment in Paris. *November 1974*: in Avignon, protests by hundreds of undocumented Moroccan seasonal workers. *December 1974*: major protest movement for permits throughout the Vaucluse region. *January 1975*: hunger strike and protest by undocumented immigrants in Montpellier. *February 1975*: national gathering of immigrant workers in Montpellier. *September 1975*: protest by Mauritian workers for their regularization. *March 1979*: start of the protest campaign against the deportation of brothers Samir and Mogniss Abdallah.

Against racist crimes. *October 1971*: the murder of fifteen-year-old Djellali Ben Ali by the concierge of his building in the Goutte d'Or neighborhood triggers a major protest movement that culminates in a march by 3000 people including

2000 immigrants. *November 1972*: protests following the killing of Mohamed Diab in a police station in Versailles. *June 1972*: protest by Maghrebin workers in Lyon after the death of Rezki Arzeki. *August 1972*: a thousand immigrant workers protest in Marseille against the murder of Bekri Mohamed. *September 1973*: the killing of Lounès Ladj leads to a strike over several days in the factories of La Ciotat, which spreads to all the departments of the Bouche-du-Rhône and Var regions. On September 14, in protest against a series of racist crimes (seven in the Paris region and one in Corsica), the MTA calls for a strike by Arab workers in the Paris region that is largely followed.

Solidarity with Palestine. *September 1970*: students from Tunisia, Morocco, and Syria launch committees in support of the Palestinian revolution that are primarily active in immigrant neighborhoods and residences, for example, in Paris and Marseille. The Palestine committees quickly become organizations in the fight against racism in France and lead to the creation of the Mouvement des travailleurs arabes (Arab Workers Movement or MTA) in 1972.

Urban youth. *1979*: creation of Rock Against Police, "an experiment in national interurban coordination of young immigrants and proletarians,"[64] established in the working-class areas of the Paris region, the Lyon banlieue, and, to a lesser extent, in the northern neighborhoods of Marseille. *1980*: creation in Lyon of the Zaâma d'Banlieue association. These two years see the first revolts by young people in neighborhoods outside Lyon. In July 1981, two months after the election of Mitterrand as president of the French Republic, violent riots break out in Minguettes, Vénissieux, Villeurbanne, and Vaux-en-Velin, extending into September.

Impressive! While it may be incomplete, compiled from information gathered here and there,[65] this list is already very significant. It bears witness to the proliferation of (colonial and European) immigration struggles in the early 1970s. In all evidence, the crisis of White Power (*pouvoir*) expressed in May '68 that continued after the departure of General de Gaulle in intense social protests, also liberated Indigenous Power (*puissance*). Just a class struggle, some would say. No! Definitely not! When they go on strike even if it is only to obtain a raise in salary, the indigenous continue the decolonial struggle simply by being indigenous. The generic notions of immigrant workers or laborers hide heterogeneous social and political realities. If indigenous workers find themselves in the *social* position they occupy, generally as specialized workers in the major French companies, restricted moreover to the most demanding and dangerous jobs, it is because of their *racial* position.

Unlike the French workers and laborers from other European countries whose immigration comes from another history and another present, the indigenous find themselves here, in France, working, living in the conditions they have because of the colonization of their country of origin and the incomplete decolonialization process. "If we are here, it's because you were there!" as could be read on a Mouvement des indigènes de la république (MIR, Movement of the Indigenous of the Republic) banner during the Decolonial March of May 8, 2008. The capitalist social relation into which the indigenous are inserted includes a racial social relation in the framework of the colonial mode of oppression.

The indigenous proletariat therefore waged a decolonial struggle in companies but also against other forms of racial oppression: spatial relegation and housing conditions, lack of security in the right to work and residency, racist violence... Defensive when they rose up against new discriminatory measures implemented by the state or against the increase in racist crimes, the extreme form of white working-class resistance, these struggles also took the offensive when they endeavored to protest the special treatment that France had long reserved for its indigenous workforce. The rise of immigrant resistance incited other forms of organization, of which the MTA was undoubtedly the most political and radical expression: Fédération des travailleurs d'Afrique noire immigrés, Comité des travailleurs algériens, Union des travailleurs immigrés tunisiens, Association des travailleurs marocains, Mouvement des sans-papiers mauritiens, Mouvement des travailleurs ivoiriens, and the creation of the Maison des travailleurs immigrés (MTI) in Paris housing different immigrant associations.[66] Finally, on the cusp of the 1980s, new actors entered the scene, occupied the political space, and changed it profoundly: the children of immigration.

As indigenous struggles proliferated and found often substantial support from the post-May '68 far left or from the humanist and Christian left (I will return to it later), the White Power counterattacked. First in living spaces, where solidarity was built and rancor fermented. Shantytowns were quickly demolished (the last one disappeared in 1976) and dedicated lodgings were developed. They would become "cités de transit et d'urgence," transitional and emergency housing projects officially designed to allow access to social housing after a period of formatting and adaptation of the indigenous to the dominant norms of individual, collective, and housing life.[67] The Republic obviously did not mention racial conflicts but rather the difficult cohabitation of culturally different communities. The Circular of April 19, 1972 therefore defined these "cités de transit" as "housing designated as provisional lodging for precarious families whose access to definitive housing cannot be considered without socio-educational action aimed at encouraging their social insertion and their promotion." The indigenous were placed under the supervision of a manager who was responsible for indicating any "poor behavior" to social assistants. The savages had to learn order. And besides, the less of them the better! Already, "in a report submitted to the Economic and Social Council in February 1969, Corentin Calvez, general secretary of the General Confederation of Executives, discussed the notion of a 'threshold of tolerance' in schools and in housing."[68] This notion, which has been at the heart of subsequent immigration policies, became a subject of controversy in 1974 when the French Institute for Demographic Studies, or INED, tried to measure the "threshold of tolerance" of French society in regard to foreigners. Although it was not put in these exact terms, the idea was also present in the Programme habitat et vie sociale (Habitat and Social Life Plan) of 1977, which posited that above a certain percentage of the population, the presence of people resulting from immigration in a neighborhood would lead to conflicts in cohabitation and to urban and social disintegration. We will see later how this same logic underpins the plans promoting "social diversity." Too many indigenous or, in other words, an increase in indigenous social power represents a threat to the white order. The immigrant labor force was so indispensable to the proper functioning of the economic machine that importing them had to be accepted, but as soon as it rebelled, as soon as it no longer accepted behaving as the mere labor force it was supposed to be, then these damaged goods had to be returned to sender, the new arrivals had to be tightly screened, and useless mouths had to be suppressed, since they "reproduce like rats," to use the lovely words of Oriana Fallaci.

In the early 1970s, it was not yet clear that the economic recession—which started to appear even before the first "oil crisis"—would be a lasting one. Employers had an inkling, as they were more concerned with their profits than the color of France. White Power spread, but the apparent unruliness of the indigenous worried it as protector of order and of racial order. In addition to the offensive carried out to heighten the supervision of immigrants by the state, through the establishment of transitional and new housing, there was a battery of measures aimed at destabilizing the indigenous labor force, reducing the flow of immigration, and instituting greater control over entry and residency conditions. Adopted in 1972, the Marcellin-Fontanet

Circulars were welcomed by the major labor unions, which were particularly sensitive to white working-class pressure. Already strict, they were only a bare outline of the structures that would later be adopted. In particular, the CNPF (National Council of French Employers) allowed a certain flexibility in their application. It is also true that the immigration question was important but not yet a leading political issue. Despite this status, it was already being discussed during the 1974 campaign, not by Jean-Marie Le Pen, who was only a "minor candidate" without influence,[69] but by the winner of the presidential election, Valéry Giscard d'Estaing. As soon as he was elected, he designated a Secretary of State for the condition of immigrant workers, Paul Dijoud. By July, the government decided to suspend the immigration of foreign workers and their families,[70] this time with the agreement of business executives who had been shaken by the oil embargo decided in October 1973 by the Arab member states of OPEC. The CGT and FO (General Confederation of Labor and Workers' Force) had no objections. Only the CFDT (French Democratic Confederation of Labor), which was strongly leftist at the time, condemned the border closings.

Of course, screening was also important. The main target of this policy was postcolonial immigration, primarily from Algeria, and then immigration from Sub-Saharan Africa starting in the years 1974–1975. As Alexis Spire observes, "Like the structure aimed at Algerians established a few years earlier, the existence of a special dispensation applied by specialized agents only for this immigration from black Africa supported a process of stigmatization at all levels of the prefectural hierarchy."[71] He also notes that the restrictive measures of the July 1974 circular made an exception for "asylum seekers and refugees, as well as foreign nationals of certain Southeast Asian countries, the spouses of French citizens, citizens of European Community nations, and finally highly skilled workers."[72] Portuguese and Spanish were also victims of discrimination and measures aimed at reducing immigration; however, "recognized as future Europeans,"[73] to use Patrick Weil's expression, they also avoided many of these restrictions.

At the end of 1975, reforms made conditions stricter for allocating work permits. A few months later, family reunification was temporarily authorized under certain circumstances but then prohibited again in 1977. This same year, Lionel Stoleru, the new Secretary of State for the condition of immigrant workers, offered them a "deal": "Get out and we'll give you a ten thousand francs." "I am here, and I am staying," was the basic response of the indigenous. Giscard d'Estaing's minister did not back down. He was intent on "liberating" France of

100,000 foreigners per year. Forced returns, creation of quotas for residency permits to be distributed in each department, cancellation of residency permits in cases of unemployment for more than six months or "a late return from paid vacation"; in fact, Stoleru did not hesitate to use any means possible, to the point that some of his measures were repealed by the Constitutional Council. During his losing 1981 presidential campaign, Valéry Giscard d'Estaing estimated the "excess" immigrant labor force to number 700,000 and proposed to rid France of 250,000 foreign workers in four years.

Giscard also oversaw the start of a very colonial policy towards Islam. As they said at the top levels of government, as long as the "Mohammedans" were praying, they could not attend union meetings. While Interior Minister Michel Poniatowski mobilized law enforcement services to break up protest movements, Paul Dijoud claimed to promote immigrant "culture." He encouraged company leaders to make it easier to practice the Muslim faith, promised that Muslim "chaplains" would be able to go to prisons and hospitals, and announced arrangements for Muslim cemeteries. A national office of cultural promotion was then established, which was responsible for the "Mosaïques" television program aimed at foreign communities, among others. However, this policy was put on hold by Lionel Stoleru when he replaced Paul Dijoud at the State Secretariat for Immigration. Stoleru favored an exclusively heavy-handed approach.

Nevertheless, the government policy towards immigration remained hesitant. It came up against the resistance of immigrant workers supported by the far left, humanist Christian traditions, and even the Socialist Party, which all became the go-betweens for the growing Indigenous Political Power while annexing it for their own purposes. I will put it another way: white forces on the left participated in the rise of Indigenous Power while at the same time hindering its autonomous political development. I am by no means seeking to question the sincerity of the anti-racist commitment of many activists on the left who gave their time for immigration struggles—including, as was often the case, when this commitment veiled a certain white paternalism[74]—but only to draw attention to this paradoxical dynamic. As for the leadership of the PS (Socialist Party), however, there is little doubt about its strictly opportunistic support of immigrant workers. The Socialist Party has a heavy colonialist history. It is the product of the unification of the remnants of the former SFIO (French Section of the Workers' International) and some Republican groups under the direction of François Mitterrand, who was Interior Minister in 1954 when the show-down began in Algeria.[75] The anti-racism that the

PS later displayed was opportunistic, motivated by the desire to expand the field of competition against the Right. However, it also expressed different aims: to win over the new forces on the left that emerged after May '68 and to block the French Communist Party (PCF). The communists and their union representative, the CGT, showed themselves to be particularly reticent to defend the demands of immigrant workers. After the breakdown of the Union of the Left in the fall of 1977, they did not hesitate to become the voice of white working-class resistance.[76] Haunted by its own decline, the PCF only had one goal: sabotage the PS and its seemingly irresistible growth. The final years of Valéry Giscard d'Estaing's seven-year term were marked by increased competition within White Power. On the Right, the Gaullists led by Jacques Chirac were determined to steal a march on Giscard d'Estaing, even if it meant allowing the Left to win the presidency in 1981. On the left, the PCF was determined to let the Right win the election as long as the Socialist Party suffered. The Communist Party had advanced its goal by withdrawing abruptly from the Union of the Left on the eve of the legislative elections of 1978; three years later, however, Mitterrand triumphed. Giscard d'Estaing would not recover, and neither would the PCF.

5

From Marronage to Jihad: The Metamorphoses
of Indigenous Power

*"I may take flight, but all the while I am fleeing, I
will be looking for a weapon!"*
　　　　—George Jackson, *Soledad Brother*, 1970

The *Marche pour l'égalité et contre le racisme*
(March for Equality and Against Racism) in
December 1983 made a lot of noise at the time
before falling into the dustbin of French memory.
Few today, including us, remember it. Some, however, keep a few traces in their mind. What was it?
The "March of the *beurs*,"[77] a "great moment of
fraternity," the emergence of SOS Racism? We no
longer know exactly. Some have turned it into a
myth, forgetting the immigration struggles that
paved the way for it. It has become impossible to
highlight its limits without taking the risk of a
beating. Others are more disillusioned or strictly
uncompromising: for them, the March was only

a giant spectacle, controlled from afar by the presidential palace or manipulated by the Left. Many who were often actors or direct witnesses of the protests in the 1980s critique it in terms of its later consequences, which they grasp with undeserved severity. Rather than approaching this event from the perspective of the—necessarily long and contradictory—history in which it was inscribed, they interpret it in a biased way through their own deceived hopes, the defeats suffered, the (relative, in my opinion) failure of political and organizational projects that they themselves supported or in which they believed.

The March, however, represented a major turning point, a historic shift: it was the start of a new era. There had of course been larger protest marches in France since 1968, larger than this march that assembled 100,000 people by favorable estimates; there had been other conflicts and some much more spectacular social crises. The only result had been makeshift institutional reforms. Even when fought by political parties, the largest struggles were union struggles in the end, inscribed in the continuity of the republic. Generally polarized around the question of redistribution of wealth, they only rarely or marginally contested the political foundation of the republican pact. So-called "social" conflicts sometimes mobilized large numbers of people and they led to cultural, ideological, and social transformations that should not be over-looked. Nevertheless, these evolutions seem to resemble aftershocks of the upheaval caused by the great political crisis of May-June 1968 more than the new ruptures. Looking back twenty-five years later, Mitterrand's election in May 1981 did not represent the historic event that many have called it. The long transition period carried out in state organizations by the teams on the left that replaced politicians and other technocrats on the right ensured the continuity of the Republic as they were hesitant to shake up the institutions put in place by de Gaulle. While the Socialists' rise to power profoundly remodeled the political field, this renewal, whether you regret it or celebrate it, may only have been to the extent that it accelerated the decline of the Communist Party and, more generally, contributed to the dissolution of the independent political power of the working class and its potential for calling into question the republican pact, or at least some of its aspects.

To quote Sayad, "the eruption onto the public stage, and therefore into the political arena, of the youth of immigration" was *in itself* the vector for an upheaval in the political field. It represented, he added, "undoubtedly, the essential event of this penultimate decade of the century." It "marks a break"[78] because "the demand for 'civil rights,' the demand for political commitment in the full sense of the word and, consequently, for moving onto the properly political terrain of struggles that traditionally were confined to the space conceded to immigrants, in other words the struggles directly related to work and waged under the banner of labor, is taken up almost everywhere."[79] It "marks a break" because it creates the awareness that "the defense of immigrants, the improvement of their conditions, and support them on every level can no longer be ensured today unless they are situated deliberately and openly in the political field, unless immigrants themselves, and especially their children engage with it directly and commit their action to the political sphere."[80] Without a clear political project, without organization, and only immediately concerning a small minority of people, the March for Equality nevertheless emerged as the first major event since May '68 because it brought immigration into *political existence*. And this political existence *called into question the Republic* that had been built on the negation of indigenous political existence. Of course, most of the Marchers did not contest it explicitly and often claimed to adhere to its "values"; many of them could still believe that the Socialist government was different than those that preceded it, that it had the ambition of having the actions of the Republic live up to its words. However, the mobilization of tens of thousands of indigenous, followed by the complicity of hundreds of millions of others, shook, *in practice*, some of the fundamental pillars of the republican pact. The nation of France, its cultural contours, its ethno-centric identity, its relationship with the world, the frontiers of citizenship that it established, which had been hit by the *externally colonized* thirty years earlier, were plowed into by the sudden appearance of the *internally colonized* on the political scene in December 1983. The March was inseparable as an event from the indigenous resistances that it galvanized and also inseparable from the counter-offensive it triggered. It well and truly shook up and transfigured the French political field. Caught up in struggles internal to White Power since the 1960s despite the thrust from immigrant workers, the political scene once again found itself structured around its national-racial axis. Not that this axis had previously ceased to exist or to determine French political reality, but it had no longer been expressed as directly as one of the major sources of hegemonial conflict inside the borders of the Hexagon. Now, two levels of conflict overlapped and combined: the level of "traditional" or republican political struggles and the level of decolonial struggles. The March therefore represented the birth of an indigenal relationship of forces rooted immediately and lastingly in French reality in the Hexagon, the moment of crystallization of a new political materiality, a new racial relationship of forces. It was not, as many of us complained, a "missed opportunity," a defeat due to the idiots of SOS-Racisme and other Mitterrandist conspiracies, but a strong starting point, despite the aforementioned idiots and despite Socialist scheming. The March opened a new political cycle in France, one rhythmed by shorter cycles of struggles, offensives and counter-offensives, shifting fronts, periods of advance and periods of retreat or temporary ceasefires, opposing indigenous forces and white forces.

This first major indigenous offensive continued to develop into the 1990s. It first took the form of new marches on Paris (*Convergence 84 pour l'égalité*, in 1984, followed the next year by the *Marche pour les droits civiques*). Still impressive, but they assembled fewer people than the March in 1983. Some have seen it, incorrectly in my opinion, as the sign of a decline, of the damaging effect of divisions. This is not the case, even though the divergences that opposed the different indigenous poles engaged in the resistance could have certainly led to disillusionment, which is inevitable after a major mobilization movement. What definitely declined, however, was the support from movements on the left that favored the integrationist illusions found in the "March *of the beurs*." Subsequent marches, albeit stronger in their desire for political autonomy, could only break with the apparent consensus in the winter of 1983, discourage whites from engaging with the movement (to support or "reclaim" it), and raise concerns for some of our own who were still prisoners of their republican ideologies. It is always easy to say in hindsight, but I truly believe the choice of political clarity was justified, even when it led to reducing the immediate ability to mobilize. In place of the chimeric hope that a massive "unity" rally in Paris would be enough to influence politics, multiple attempts at organization, political definition, and strategic development were undertaken, and it would be wishful thinking to expect that they could progress in a linear manner or quickly advance without polemics, obstacles, or divisions. These impediments discouraged many of us, but they were inevitable as the movement had only just started and it had—and still needs—to define itself, break away from the white forces, build its own political space, its own perspective, before being able to unify in a lasting way. We should celebrate the fact that despite its youth, its recent creation, and the young age of most of its members, despite its lack of political savvy and its inexperience, despite the strong hostility it provoked, it was nonetheless able to continue to produce for at least ten years an abundance of organized frameworks of resistance and more or less informal networks capable of acting in several areas—social, political, cultural, and spiritual—and of taking action in different forms—establishment of independent movements and other associations, struggles "in the field," forays into the media sphere, electoral experiments, or attempts to infiltrate white parties.[81] What was decisive during this period was not their political hesitations, the splitting up of resistances, their inability to unify around a clear project, or the dependence of several of them on white forces. In a context of a retreat from social and political struggles in France that would last until the 1990s, it was much more their profusion, the flourishing of their forms and areas of intervention, the youth of the actors, the plethora of people directly involved in struggles who supported them briefly or only observed them sympathetically, and the spread of new ideas. Most of all, due to the fact that many indigenous entered the political field, positions resistant to the national-racial order were raised.

The white reaction was brutal. It was deployed on a wide variety of fronts and developed different strategies of containment. The momentum of the March started to fade in the 1990s. It left our memory. Often, the younger brothers and sisters of the Marchers no longer believed in anything, as they were floored by the economic, social and police violence in neighborhoods. The areas of struggle that had gained the most visibility unraveled, crumbled; many were subjugated in the periphery of White Power, cronyism, taken hostage, or simply, gradually, shackled by the many compromises necessary for the survival of some activities; the networks came undone; countless militants were discouraged, resigned to putting on their slippers or to being hunched over the organization of local resistance in fragmented but vital causes; the efforts of political clarification dried up; and the accumulated experience was squandered. All of this is true but only to a certain extent: the extent that political progress is understood as a continuous accumulation of strength and not like breathing. There is little doubt that there were defeats, retreats, and a certain loss of substance starting in the 1990s. Yet these terms are overly unilateral. They leave out an entire aspect of reality. They are distorted by the tendency to see the progress of power relations only through notions of events, of what is supposed to be "news" in the prism of the white media's selective view, for whom the *real news* of immigrants or their children, their struggles and their resistance remain largely invisible.

Instead of lamenting the breakdown of some forms of indigenous struggle, we should emphasize the shifts in resistance, the multiplication of fronts, and the appearance of new meanings. The attempts to establish a unified force of immigration and its descendants failed but, in truth, the opposite would have been surprising, given the youth of the movement. It is important, however, that these attempts were constantly renewed. Some dynamics of the struggle grew weaker, such as the dynamic of immigrant workers after the major automobile strikes of 1983–1984, which resembled the general struggles of the working class. Other dynamics took over, like the struggle of undocumented immigrants that, despite difficulties and setbacks, has started over and over again since the major protests of 1996 until today.

My aim is not to give a general overview of indigenous resistance or to relive its history but simply to draw attention to some of the lines of force in the—difficult—constitution of an Indigenous Power within hexagonal France and the changes that have characterized it over the past two decades.

The main focal point of this power is indisputably the indigenous neighborhoods. The attempts made at political organization in these areas have always been hesitant and weak, centered around local action, and seldom capable of inspiring mass popular action. However, we should not underestimate the multiplicity and diversity of the spaces and forms of resistance that have developed there since the 1980s. They have generally been articulated around demands related to the special treatment reserved for the populations resulting from colonization who live in housing blocks. Police brutality and harassment, racism, housing access and conditions, unemployment, discrimination at school, limited municipal infrastructure, religious segregation against Muslims, de facto restrictions on the right to association, exclusion from representative bodies, deportation, and double penalties are all issues that often led to more or less lasting spaces for structured protests. The white counteroffensive on the national and local scale, the intent to bribe the leaders of new associations, to muzzle, stifle, and marginalize the most rebellious spaces of resistance had even more visibly detrimental effects. However, they did not eliminate all solidarity, they did not extinguish the deep revolt of the youth of the housing projects or restrict all forms of organized protest.

Associations and networks created in the wake of the March, like the Jeunes arabes de Lyon et banlieues (JALB, Young Arabs of Lyon and Suburbs) founded in 1985, pursued their activities for a time; others appeared like the *Résistance des banlieues* network, established in 1989 in the perspective of coordinating spaces for struggle in the housing projects. The first "Conference of Youth from the *Banlieues*," held in February 1992 in Lyon, also represented an important moment of convergence. The incursions into the domain reserved for electoral representation should also be mentioned, in particular in the establishment of autonomous lists for various municipal elections. Probably because it was able to siphon off the most white support,[82] the protest against "double penalties" received the most media attention. Launched in 1986 with the "*J'y suis, j'y reste*" (I am here, I am staying) campaign, started by the JALB, Résistance des banlieues, the Sol'Act association,[83] in 1990, and the Comité national contre la double peine (National Committee Against the Double Penalty) that later became the Mouvement de l'immigration et des banlieues (MIB, Immigration and *Banlieues* Movement), this fight reached its peak in 1992–1993 and continued even while losing momentum until the end of the decade. While the double penalty was not abolished, the protests made it possible to restrict its field of application. I could cite numerous other associations that emerged in the wake of these struggles, like Agora and DiverCités, in the Lyon region. Indigenous resistance in the banlieues was also found a flourishing cultural and artistic expression, of which the most notable forms were found in linguistic inventiveness and the wave of anti-establishment rap and hip-hop. Often recuperated by the dominant white society, rap is nonetheless the sign of the dynamic resistance of neighborhoods; even today, it represents one of the main forms of media through which powerfully anti-colonial cultural and political ties are created in new generations, especially indigenous ones.

While the associative movement emerging from the fights of the 1980s was inarguably weakened in the 1990s, it did not result in an overall collapse of Indigenous Power. The multiple revolts—or riots, the term used does not matter—in working-class neighborhoods over the past twenty years is clearly the sign of dramatic deficiencies in terms of organizations; they nevertheless represent a form of resistance with a real impact on political power relations. The most memorable are the first revolts in the summer of 1981, the revolt in October 1990 in Vaulx-en-Velin, and of course the national revolt of November 2005. In fact, the riots and confrontations with law enforcement have continued almost uninterrupted over the past two decades, mostly in reaction to police involvement in the death of neighborhood youths, most often—oddly enough!—black or Arab. Our memory only retains a few emblematic events that made the front page; White Power records their succession and deploys numerous strategies to counter them. Here again, certain episodes are worth remembering. I will refer below to the chronology established by the group Les mots sont importants (LMSI, Words Are Important) that I have reproduced almost in its entirety.[84]

March 1991: riots in the Cité des Indes housing estate in Sartrouville (Yvelines) following the death of 18-year-old Djamel Chettouh, who was killed in a mall by a security guard. *May*: violent incidents in the Val-Fourré area of Mantes-la-Jolie (Yvelines) after the death of Aïssa Ihiche, age 18, while in custody in the town's police station. *June*: strong protests after the killing of Youssef Khaïf, age 23, shot in the neck by Officer Pascal Hiblot in Mantes-la-Jolie. The officer was acquitted in September 2001. *November 1993*: riots in Melun (Seine-et-Marne), after the death of a boy from the Nord neighborhood of the city. *February 1994*: riots in the Sapins neighborhood in the heights of Rouen after the death of Ibrahim Sy, an 18-year-old Senegalese youth killed by a gendarme while in a stolen vehicle. *March*: incidents between youth and law enforcement in Garges-lès-Gonesse (Val'd'Oise), after the death of 16-year-old Philippe Huynh, and in the Tramontane neighborhood of the Avignon banlieues following the death of Mohammed Tajira, age 17. *September*: skirmishes between youth and police in Pau in the Ousse-des-Bois neighborhood following the killing of Azzouz Read, age 24. *May 1995*: incidents in Le Havre after the death of Belkacem Belhabib, age 23, at the end of a police chase. *September*: confrontations between youth and police break out in the Cité des Fontenelles housing estate in Nanterre

(Hauts-de-Seine) after the death of Nouredine Benomari, age 25. *November*: riots in the Saint-Nicolas neighborhood of Laval after the death of Abdelkader Bouziane, age 16, shot in the head by officers of the anti-criminality brigade (BAC); incidents in Lyon in the Duchère neighborhood after the death of Fabrice Fernandez, age 24, in a police station; riots in the Strasbourg housing projects on New Year's eve: fifty cars burned in one night. *December 1998*: several nights of riots enflamed the neighborhoods of Toulouse after the death of Habib Ould Mohamed, age 17, killed by a police officer during an attempted interrogation. *May 1999*: riots in Vauvert (Gard) following the death of Mounir Oubbaja, age 19, struck down by a local inhabitant. *September 2000*: skirmishes in the housing estates of Grand-Borne in Grigny (Essonne) and Tarterêts in Corbeil-Essonnes after the death of Ali Rezgui, age 19, killed by a police officer in Combs-la-Ville (Seine-et-Marne) when forcing through a barricade in a small van. *July 2001*: incidents broke out in the Borny housing projects of Metz after the death of two neighborhood youths. *October*: violent clashes between law enforcement and youths in Thonon-les-Bains (Haute-Savoie) after the accidental death of four young people from a housing estate who were attempting to evade a police check. *December*: several nights of rioting struck Vitry-sur-Seine

(Val-de-Marne) after the death of a young man from the La Dalle Robespierre housing estate, killed by the police during a holdup. *January 2002*: incidents at the Les Musiciens housing estate in Les Mureaux (Yvelines) after the death of Moussa, age 17, killed by a police officer while trying to break through a barricade on the peripheral road. *February*: clashes between youths and law enforcement in Évreux (Eure) after the overdose death of a young drug addict inside the police station. *October*: violent riots in the Hautepierre neighborhood of Strasbourg following the drowning death of a 17-year-old from the housing estate who was attempting to escape police after being surprised during the burglary of a warehouse. *January 2004*: 324 cars burned in different cities of France during the night of January 1: violent clashes took place in particular between young people and the CRS in the Neuhof neighborhood of Strasbourg; riots in the Hautepierre housing project after the death of a young 19 year old, struck on a stolen motorcycle while attempting to escape the police. *October 2005*: while visiting a neighborhood of Argenteuil (Val-d'Oise), Nicolas Sarkozy was called out by a group of young people whom he then called "scum" and "gangrene." Riots broke out in Clichy-sous-Bois (Seine-Saint-Denis) after the electrocution of three young men in an EDF transformer as they attempted to escape the police. Two of them died.

November: aggravation of the violence in Clichy-sous-Bois. Car burning and clashes with law enforcement progressively spread throughout Seine-Saint-Denis and to several French cities. On the 8th, the government declared a state of emergency that remained in effect until January 2006. Calm returned in mid-November. *May 2006*: violent brawls between young people and law enforcement in Montfermeil (Seine-Saint-Denis)—as well as Clichy-sous-Bois—after a "muscular" raid carried out by police in the Bosquets housing estate. *November 2007*: new riots in Villiers-le-Bel.

Whatever they may have said themselves, in the slogans, the demands made, and the immediate causes that provoked them, these riots come from resistance to the colonial policy implemented in neighborhoods, especially in terms of police management. The national revolt in November 2005 was in this sense an *anti-colonialist revolt*. From the perspective that concerns us here, it matters little that the words used by the actors of this revolt did not explicitly challenge the system of indigenous status. Or that the social causes related to economic liberalization could also have been a fertile terrain for discontent. This revolt was a protest in action, bringing together indigenous and whites against the indigenization of the working-class suburbs that had been carried out by different governments for years. The colonialist reaction that followed, starting with the establishment of a curfew, borrowed directly from the colonial arsenal of repression, and ending with the racist vote that gave Sarkozy an electoral victory is further proof.

The shift in resistance also took the form of cultural self-affirmation in the face of republican racism and assimilationism. Speaking of the involvement of MTA militants in the anti-racism fight, assembled to a large extent in solidarity with the Palestinian people, Mogniss Abdallah described it as the development in the West of the "anti-Arab racist propaganda" that followed "the Arab defeat in the June 1967 war."[85] We can reverse this proposition to explain the enthusiasm Arab youth in France showed for the Palestinian cause. The anti-Arab and Islamophobic escalation in the West that has continued to grow since the 1980s and has been actively promoted by the political, media, and intellectual representatives of the Zionist state, pushed these youths to see the murderous aggression descending on the Arabs and Muslims of Palestine or elsewhere as the same racist oppression to which they were subjected on a daily basis. In other words, their support for Palestinian, Lebanese, Iraqi, and other peoples was not simply "international solidarity" as practiced by some movements of the radical white left. Nor is it a pure "ethnic" identification as some have written. It is the often unspoken awareness that the anti-colonialist fight of the Palestinian Arabs and the anti-racist fight of the Arabs in France have the same enemy: Western domination. Palestine for us is not an imaginary substitute for a "lost or imagined homeland," as Esther Benbassa asserts in lumping together both Zionist activists and pro-Palestinian militants. Supporting the Palestinians means supporting themselves as indigenized Arabs. Declaring to white faces that "I am Arab!," "I am Muslim!," "I support Arabs because they are Arabs and Muslims because they are Muslim!," is not essentially defending an "ethnicity." It means: "We the people who are victims of racism and colonialism, we are united by a common fate." It is an eminently political declaration. Manifesting solidarity with the Palestinian people, asserting one's Arabness and Islamicness, holding on to a culture that the racist Republic seeks to eradicate all come from the same intention.

I do not think I have drifted too far from the topic at hand; I only wanted to emphasize two things, or actually three. The first, that the pro-Palestinian commitment of the new indigenous generations is fundamentally a fight against racism in France; second, that this solidarity, far from shrinking, increasingly represents one of the vectors through which Indigenous Power is realized as an autonomous political power; third, that, without being

the only reason, it is concomitant and often identified with this other form of anti-colonial resistance
expressed on cultural and spiritual levels.

In fact, the dislocation of the political axis from
resistance starting in the 1990s notably took the
form of cultural affirmation through a Muslim
frame of reference. A *jihad* was started to regain
self-control. The motivations specific to each individual on the spiritual level belong only to them. It
is utterly indecent to judge them in any way.
However, as soon as religious inspiration becomes
a large-scale collective phenomenon and takes on
political implications, it becomes vital to understand its scope. It is true that in the context of the
colonial relationship, and to the extent that it can
express an effort at self-reappropriation through
the search of the divine, the spiritual tension of the
indigenous is not entirely disconnected from the
political in that it induces a collision with the
forces that attempt to tear the indigenous away
from themselves to subject them to the norms of
the white Republic. In this way, it is already a form
of resistance to racial oppression. What concerns
us here, however, is the overall, probably political
signification of the return to the Islamic faith and
practices in France. For twenty years, white
researchers and journalists—to whom we must add
the different police and intelligence services—
dedicated quantities of publications and studies to

the complexity of an expanding "Islamic land-scape" in France. Most of the time with concern and malice. At best, they wanted to be reassuring: Muslims, even the most practicing ones, are not bad; they are on the path to quick "integration." With words borrowed from the traditional vocabulary of Islam, the nice white people say, Muslims are happy to express the "universal values" of "modernity." As long as the Republic shows itself to be tolerant and open, as long as a real "dialogue of cultures" is established, well then, France has nothing to fear, "national cohesion" will be ensured, and we will all move together towards "progress." A paternalistic vision expressed in its most caricatural form by some militants on the left opposed to the prohibition on wearing the veil in school: if the Republic allows schoolgirls to wear veils, they basically asserted, they would end up wearing miniskirts and send their fathers, brothers, cousins, and other macho neighbors packing. In truth, the whites professing tolerance were wrong. Not when they were expressing their faith in the ability of the Republic to absorb individuals individually, but in its capacity to incorporate the collective phenomenon of French Islam with equality, as one of its constitutive dimensions. Founded on a national-racial, white-European-Christian pact, the Republic can only conceive of relations with Muslim communities under the form of a hierarchical relationship like the one that characterized the former colonies. In this white-Christian republic, the massive presence of Muslims considering themselves as Muslims contradicts the Republican pact. I say it without hesitation: an indigenous Muslim voting in municipal elections for a Sarkozy candidate who has promised to build a mosque is much more of a problem for the Republic than a secular indigenous voter who votes Socialist in the legislative elections in the hope that the Socialists will increase wages. Shock! Accusations: "He's telling people to vote Sarkozy!" And no, I don't like the UMP that much, go figure. Or the PS. I can't stand either one. They both participate in White Power and, with sometimes different strategies, both aim to break our resistance and instrumentalize us in the competition between them. I am only trying to unravel how, through contradictory and sometimes aberrant mediations, an indigenous politics takes form.

Like all forms of resistance, necessarily affected or even fashioned by the oppression that elicit them, the Muslim expansion in France today is, of course, necessarily ambivalent. It is also connected to other issues that thwart its subversive potential. It is not always capable of expressing itself outside the apparatuses of the most powerful French Muslim organizations whose particular interests often intersect with the interests of some Arab states—concerned with keeping control of "their" immigration or having a potential means to pressure the French state—since they are implicated in the issues of a White Power that is increasingly tempted to use Islamic "clergy" to maintain its domination, like the strategy used in its former colonies. The Union des jeunes musulmans (UJM, Union of Young Muslims UJM), created in Lyon in 1987, the Collectif des muslumans de France (CMF, French Muslim Collective), launched in 1992, the association of Étudiants musulumans de France (EMF, Muslim Students of France), created in 1989, the Union des organisations islamiques de France (UOIF, Union of Islamic Organizations of France), the large federation established in 1983, and so many other organizations that have appeared or developed since the end of the 1980s often have had different or even incompatible projects. They organize diverse generations and communities; they sometimes contribute to their separation; they are more or less independent from White Power; they focus their activities on the cultural domain or are active in social and political domains; they favor compromise or contestation; and they have disparate religious, ideological, and political references. As a whole, however, the fundamental dynamic of expansion of Islam and Muslim organizations in France shakes the foundations of the Republic and *tends* to contribute to strengthening Indigenous Political Power. Those of us who separate the different movements in French Islam between "reactionaries" and "modernists" or "progressives," using the categories that justified the "civilizing mission," are on the wrong track. The scale of "values" through which it seems pertinent to evaluate not the religious but political approach of each Muslim organization is one that makes it possible to measure the sometimes paradoxical and shifting relationship that this approach maintains with the decolonial dynamic. Or, to put it another way, without losing sight of the reality of their entanglement in the concrete conditions we still have today, it is appropriate to understand the politics of Muslim organizations using the categories of *integrationism* and *liberation* in the same way as in all our spaces of resistance. The Republic, moreover, is perfectly aware of it. Whether the interpretation of Islam promoted by the different Islamic institutions is "fundamentalist, "republican," or "progressive," according to the categories generally used, is less important than their disposition to be inserted into state structures and to contribute to keeping Muslims "in their place."

These movements, or at least the most political ones, continue to call for equal rights and treatment in an integrationist perspective that refuses to examine the republican matrix explicitly. Most only demand the right to practice their religion like the members of all other faiths. However, the dynamic of this demand tends to transgress republican limits constantly. Islam, in the French context, is not one belief among others. It cannot be reduced solely to fasting for a month or pilgrimages to Mecca. It is a cultural fact that deeply shakes the implicit foundations of the nation and public space, articulated—despite the secular concept of *laïcité*—around the place of the church; it counteracts France's insertion in Euro-Christian space by having it penetrated by another space, the space of the Muslim world. Islam is both the identity of the colonized and one of the constitutive signs of the racial boundary that encloses a fraction of the population in a dominated statutory group, in other words that produces them as social races. The demand for equal rights, even when this demand is expressed in the language of the Republic and integration, tends to strain the racial borders. In 1986, Jean Daniel wrote in *Le Nouvel Observateur*: "France is the scene of an exciting wager: transforming Islam through contact with French civilization."[86] Renan said the same thing, albeit more frankly: "The regeneration of the inferior or bastard races by the superior races is in the providential order of humanity."[87] And the leftist editorialist is indeed speaking of a "civilizing mission"; every shade of this same racism is expressed in the commentaries of French politicians and intellectuals—in most of them, unfortunately—and it comes through in the media's enthusiasm for "moderate Muslims" and other "modernizers" of Islam. When they glorify the "exciting wager" of an *aggiornamento* of Islam today, the goal of narrow-minded Islamophobes is simply to reassert the superiority of the white race, to consecrate the parameters of "French" or "European" or "Christian civilization" as a rampart against Muslims. They know that the wager at stake in the emergence of Islam in France is on the contrary the transformation of "French civilization" in contact with Islam. Or, to put it more precisely, in political terms, what worries them is the blurring of the racial borders of the Republic resulting from the expansion of French Islam. It is the reason why the strengthening of Indigenous Power, reinvigorated by Muslim action, must be seen as one of the fundamental causes of this retreat to the Republic, "French secularity," and the nation. In the same way, if the anti-"communitarian" hysteria reveals something, it is the fear that indigenous people might aspire for collective liberation and not individual emancipation alone, which is necessarily integrationist, that they are not content with challenging the dominant norms imposed on individuals but might come to question the institutional principles of the Republic. A fear that is not completely unjustified. Of course, no Muslim, or more generally, no indigenous organization is demanding specific collective rights today. Legal equality between abstract individuals—the republican "value" that masks the persistent reality of communities or groups granted unequal rights—is not contested by anyone as foundation of the laws, citizenship, and institutions of the state. The "regionalist" claims that appeared in the 1970s already shook the foundations of the "One and Indivisible" Jacobin national Republic. Our organizations, however, have strongly rejected them. Out of integrationist conviction or not to provide ammunition to their adversaries, the indigenous often call on the sacred principles of the Republic. Many of them, even if they have been French for years, continue to consider themselves illegitimate. They forbid themselves from discussing the "values" of France and even more from *remaking* France. Only the "real owners" of France, the white, European, Christian French, the "*souchiens*,"[88] would have the right to say what is sacred or not. As for us, we could only call for our insertion into the structures of legal equality (abstract equality of "chances"), while bowing before the French flag. Except that the "three colors" are not merely the symbol of legal equality, they are also an affirmation of the hierarchy of racial groups. Legal equality carries in itself both real inequality and real equality. The first as its form of concrete existence, the second as virtual political reality that supposes the negation of the first. When Muslims call for the recognition of Islam as collective culture of a fraction of the population, in the strict framework of the legal equality of individuals, they constantly surpass the limits of this framework, which is based on the negation of group interests, collective cultures, and on the statutory inferiority of Islam. In other words, while it remains caught in the web of integrationism, the call for the legal equality for Muslims carries the demand for real equality, which contains the desire to live collectively, to be represented institutionally as they are, and to participate in the very definition of the nation. It is an intolerable demand from the perspective of the national-racial Republic. When republicans question the "compatibility" of Islam with the Republic, they are merely admitting the Republic's incompatibility with Muslims.

Far from being a step backwards in relation to the March of 1983, as some think, the expansion of Islam prolongs it, by both continuing it and breaking with it. It carries an unprecedented subversive charge. It shifts indigenous resistance in relation to the republican right-left split that prevented it from thinking for itself and constructing its own political autonomy. One could object, of course, that the major Muslim organizations are now participating in the structures of White Power. The potential dynamic of Muslim demands seems much more important to me. Without question, the policies of UOIF leadership, to only cite one example, aim in particular to ensure its own hold over Muslims in the context of working with the state; from this point of view, it is hindering the development of all the virtual possibilities of Indigenous Power. At the same time, however, the hundreds of thousands of indigenous that come each year to the Bourget Air Show are performing an act of resistance no matter what their individual motives. Am I repeating myself? I have to. The construction of the Conseil français du culte musluman (CFCM, French Council of the Muslim Religion), a bureaucratic apparatus for controlling Islam, can only be explained as a reaction to the destabilizing potential of indigenous power. Without clearly designing an anti-integrationist policy, Muslims adopt an anti-integrationist approach by developing cultural differences, asserting themselves as a collective body and, why not, as "communitarianists." Even though it is not expressed in terms of political protest, even though we do not see vast protests and strikes by Muslims, and even though there are not yet Muslim candidates draining hundreds of thousands of votes in elections, the increase in the number of mosques,

beards, and veils represents a major political phenomenon, a flagrant defeat of the "*beur*-ization"
strategy aimed at the children of immigration.
This Islam comes from the movement of consolidation of Indigenous Political Power. Eminently
contradictory? Yes, but the same is true for all
indigenous resistance (and every struggle of the
dominated). Its historical signification never
comes from before but belongs to the future; it will
be the fruit of changes in power relations. Its
future will depend on the emergence or not of a
decolonial political leadership.

The issue of culture as mediation of the racial
question also represented one of the major forms
of radicalization of the other indigenous from the
overseas departments (DOMs) residing in France,
also known as "*Domiens.*" While Africans, North
Africans, and Domiens sometimes came together
in companies and indigenous neighborhoods
during protests, in the rest of the political space,
they have mostly followed separate but parallel
paths. Until recently, Afro-Maghreb immigration
and immigration from the overseas colonial territories seemed to correspond to different political
issues. From this point of view, maybe indirectly,
the March for Equality undoubtedly had an
important impact on Antillean resistance, the
major axis of overseas resistance in France.

Nevertheless, they followed a progression that was symmetrical to postcolonial immigration. In the 1960s, the death of the plantation economy, the rural exodus that followed, deepening social differentiations benefitting the Békés (descendants of European settlers in the Antilles), poverty, and unemployment forced many Antilleans to seek better conditions in metropolitan France. However, in addition to this phenomenon that was in many respects analogous to postcolonial immigration from the Maghreb or Sub-Saharan Africa, there was a policy to transfer authority from the Antilles to France through various institutional structures like the well-known Bumidon (Office for Migrations Involving Overseas Departments), created in 1961. There were several reasons for these policies, in particular the fear that social trouble and revolts, like the ones in Martinique in 1959 and Guadeloupe in 1967, would lead to anticolonialist radicalization. The Gaullist minister Michel Debré uttered this gem in January 1972: "The direct consequence of stopping emigration is a revolutionary situation."[89] The Antillean population therefore grew fifteen times greater in less than fifty years. There are now hundreds of thousands definitively settled in France, and even more, including their descendants. Contrary to foreigners, Antilleans were able to apply for civil service jobs where the majority have, even today, been relegated to the lowest levels of the work hierarchy. Under the presidency of Valéry Giscard d'Estaing, the immigration policy was adjusted, just as it was for Arabs and Africans. Their situation then became sensibly worse, leading to union mobilizations, often marked by the articulation of specific demands related to the improvement of living conditions in France and demands related to the economic and social development of the Antilles. The first major protest took place on April 8, 1976 with the main slogan: "Antillais, Guyanais, Réunionnais, dans l'Action, Arrachons nos revendications."[90] Other fights followed in July 1977 and February 1978, showing the progress in the protests. As in the case of the movements driven by Maghrebian and African workers, the main labor unions only supported them hesitantly if at all. The attempts to exert pressure from the inside of the workers' confederations met with the indifference or racism of leadership, leading many Antillean and overseas workers to organize on their own. Starting in the late 1970s, the number of community-based associations grew. In 1980, they were three times more than in 1975; there were more than 800 in 1987.[91] From there, as the space of social demands shrank with economic restructuring and the general retreat of the labor movement, the axis of Antillean mobilization was progressively reshaped around cultural, racial, and/or anti-colonial self-determination. As Blacks, descendants of enslaved Africans, or Creoles, the Domiens endeavored to rediscover, rehabilitate, and enrich their cultural heritage, in particular in the domain of musical creation. They rebuilt the connection with Africa and/or claimed the Creole identity; they reappropriated the history of slavery and the memory of anti-slavery resistances; they mobilized for the official recognition of the crimes of France under slavery; and they demanded reparations. All these struggles culminated in the vast protest on May 23, 1998 that brought together 40,000 people in Paris. The Domien indigenous movement remains fragmented into multiple leanings and associations; the clearly anti-colonialist movements are in the minority as integrationism remains very present; resistance is often thought of in terms of lobbies instead of independent political action; some of its components participate in the networks of White Power. Despite these strong regressive tendencies, however, the overall dynamic of Domien resistance in France continues to be on the rise and participates in the general growth of Indigenous Political Power.

I obviously cannot end this chapter without mentioning the publication in January 2005 of the Public Appeal, the Appel des Indigènes de la République that led to the creation of MIR,[92] not by chance around the same time as the revolts in working-class neighborhoods in November of the same year. The contribution of this movement is not found in its ability to act and mobilize, which remains weak despite its clear influence, but primarily in the colonial/postcolonial issues that it has systematized or more precisely "precipitated" in it like a chemical reaction produced by the synthesis of the trends active below the surface of the prior experience of struggle of all the indigenous populations in France. I have already discussed the main MIR theses in another place (*Pour une politique de la racaille* (Paris: Textuel, 2006)). I will not revisit them except to mention that they began a reading of contemporary French and global reality as a renewed process of colonial domination and reproduction of racial fractures, opening the perspective of a decolonial convergence of the different indigenous communities of France.

6

How the Strategic Unity of
White Power Was Built

> *"Colonial subjects have their political decisions made for them by the colonial masters, and those decisions are handed down directly or through a process of 'indirect rule.' Politically, decisions which affect black lives have always been made by white people—the "white power structure." There is some dislike for this phrase because it tends to ignore or oversimplify the fact that there are many centers of power, many different forces making decisions. Those who raise that objection point to the pluralistic character of the body politic. They frequently overlook the fact that American pluralism quickly becomes a monolithic structure on issues of race. When faced with demands from black people, the multi-faction whites unite and present a common front."*
>
> —Stokely Carmichael and
> Charles V. Hamilton, *Black Power*

The most obvious sign of the growth of Indigenous Power is unquestionably the scale of the white response opposed to it. As we have seen, it started to express itself in the early 1970s; it gained new momentum during the presidency of Valéry Giscard d'Estaing before obtaining decisive impetus in the next decade. This brief essay will not analyze all its moments or every twist and turn, nor will it propose a detailed interpretation of the policies enacted since the March for Equality. At the risk of oversimplifying, I will merely list the main stages of the construction of white consensus, insisting less on the more recent period that is fresh in our memories. In the same way, for ease of presentation, I will discuss in succession the different aspects of the white offensive. Yet it goes without saying that it is characterized by its unity. Unity of white power first, despite the arguments between its most influential parts and the tight competition between the different areas that constitute it; then the unity of its targets, the communities resulting from postcolonial immigration and the French people originally from its present colonies; unity of the means used, ideological war, repression, social and economic policies, new administrative and institutional procedures, structures of control and cronyism, and more. It took more than twenty years to build this unity on a strategic level. It is immanent to the racial character of the Republic but constantly countered by other divisions, and most recently embodied in the policies of Nicolas Sarkozy.

The majority of indigenous people who have the right to vote traditionally give their votes to the Left—more specifically the Socialist Party, reputed to be anti-racist or, in any case, less inclined to "beat up ragheads." But that would mean forgetting the heavy colonial heritage of French social democracy. It is true that during the 1970s, as the discourse of the Right on immigration hardened and the French Communist Party barely hid its inclination for "national preference," the PS did not hesitate to defend immigrant workers. Anti-racism was certainly not one of its main concerns, far from it, but in comparison with its competitors in the white political field, it had to show itself to be "humanist," with a concern for promoting equality. However, after Mitterrand became head of state, many white activists who had supported our cause refused to stand by our side. Even the sincerest among them had other priorities. And moreover, as they often thought, this new power should not be weakened by encouraging protest movements; it was enough to wait and act from within new institutions.

At first, it is true, the new government took measures that, despite their limitations, favored our resistance at first. The main acquisition of this period, the only one that was not completely or partially called into question later, is inarguably the recognition of the right for foreigners to establish associations in the framework of the Law of 1901. It was a fundamental but contradictory measure like all the republican democratic structures: it would facilitate and encourage the expression of many indigenous and *at the same time* allow state control and oversight of a branch of the associative movement, especially through the selective distribution of subsidies. The government led by the Socialists obviously did not keep all the promises it made during the campaign. It did not even revisit all the measures adopted by previous governments against immigration. It removed the "return assistance," regularized the residency of many foreigners and their families; expulsions were momentarily suspended; and other structures were loosened. The guiding principle of government policy nevertheless remained halting any new flow of migration, reinforcing border control, and strengthening penalties for immigrants in irregular situations. Very quickly, and despite the sometimes significant differences that remained between them, the Socialists adopted a policy of "firmness" towards immigration and the populations resulting from it: making the conditions for entry and residency more difficult, increased severity towards illegals, increasingly strict control of family migration, border closings, more or less disguised measures to reestablish "return assistance," and reinstatement of a 1946 decree authorizing identity checks, which were necessarily determined by physical appearance. On every level, the government established new obstacles to immigration, linking repressive measures with liberal promises. In March 1983, scarcely two years after the triumphant election of Mitterrand, the municipal election campaign traced the main axes of the upcoming white offensive: immigration, insecurity, working-class neighborhoods, and Islam.

The real turning point occurred soon after the March for Equality. As early as May 25, 1984 to be precise. For the first time, in fact, during a public debate in Parliament, the Left and the Right agreed on the strategy to take for immigration: distinguishing legal immigration to be "integrated" from illegal immigration to be suppressed. But what defines the difference between legal and illegal immigration? The law. And what would the law do? It would produce illegality. The more the possibility of legal immigration was restricted by law, the more draconian legal work and residency conditions became, the more clandestine immigration increased, the more control and repression of clandestine immigrants grew, and the more "legal" immigrants were subjected to pressure and made less secure. A policy against illegal entry is a policy against all immigration. In addition, all the populations resulting from immigration suffered its consequences at least indirectly, even if only in terms of suspicion, disparagement, and rejection.[93] The white consensus was consecrated by the law of July 14, 1984 that granted the famous ten-year card,[94] while quietly bringing back return assistance (now called "reintegration assistance") and the principle of withdrawing permits in the case of return. Laurent Fabius, the newly named Prime Minister, recognized the support of Socialists for a stronger immigration policy on this occasion. A few months later, an implementation decree ratified a series of restrictive conditions that were only made harsher by subsequent governments. On October 10, the Council of Ministers adopted a new provision to limit the right to family reunification. In the same month, thirteen administrative retention centers were opened. Commenting on the Socialist policy, Patrick Weil, the former adviser of Jean-Pierre Chevènement at the Interior Ministry, celebrated the fact that "the government on the left became aware of the fact that a certain dose of public order was necessary for the existence of the national political community."[95] Yet "public order," as we all know, is just a façade. It was much more a question of defending the white national order against immigration. Laurent Fabius admitted it implicitly when asserting, in October 1985, that he basically agreed with Jacques Chirac on the question of immigration; Jacques Chirac, the leader of an RPR and UDF alliance with a campaign platform promising: "to strengthen *national identity* by fighting *illegal* immigration." A shortcut that is also an admission: the truth of immigration policy is not to stop Arabs from "stealing French people's bread" but preserving "national identity"; the hunt for "illegals" serves as cover for the repression of all those who supposedly threaten the "national identity." Sarkozy did not invent anything. He was just more upfront about it.

This fundamental understanding between left and right would prove consistent. The Right predicted and the Left followed. In the opposition, they denounced the severity of the measures by the Right; when regaining power, they softened some provisions and replaced others that were too obviously repressive; rarely, however, did they ever call the principles into question. The operations of SOS-Racisme, which started soon after the March and as white consensus on immigration was being established, followed a complex strategy. It was of course a way to counter the Right. However, it was also, at the same time, one of the vectors of reshaping and shifting the white political field to the Right and one of the intermediaries that legitimized the alignment of the Left with the immigration policy promoted by the Right. In a certain way, which is not the least of its paradoxes, the 1983 March occurred at precisely the right moment from the perspective of a policy of "integration." And many Socialist leaders recognized it, offering conspicuous support even to the point of Mitterrand receiving a delegation of Marchers and promising them to establish the ten-year card. On a first level, it could be said that, in the context of a policy of "integration," the mediatized launch of SOS-Racisme and the "*beur*" trend that accompanied it were a way to turn the protest dynamic of the March against itself. In other words, it was a question of disguising the offensive launched against all indigenous peoples and to reassure the hierarchies that segmented them: the good "*beurs*" whom the Republic generously proposed to "integrate" and protect against the bad racists of the Front national, were therefore distinguished from their immigrant parents, too Arab to be honest,[96] and opposed to the "illegals" or more generally the "recent arrivals" who supposedly slowed the process of "integration." SOS-Racisme also piggybacked on the revolt expressed by the Marchers to impose the issues of moralizing "anti-racism" and "antifascism" on the white political field as two major issues capable of transcending the traditional divides between left and right. At a time when the Left in power renounced the famous "anti-capitalist break" that it had advocated, as the destabilizing potential of Indigenous Power was growing, a new ideological configuration took shape where the combined themes of anti-racism, tolerance, and the "right to difference" represented one of the dimensions of the broader matrix of defending the Republic, human rights, "modernity," and the fight against "exclusion." I could cite many other forms of this ideology aimed at covering the abandonment of categories of exploitation and oppression and the renunciation of a policy of social confrontation. The invention of the notion of "exclusion" complementary to the notion of "integration" is particularly significant from this perspective. There are those who are "excluded," but who are the "excluders"? What enemy needs to be conquered to eradicate "exclusion"? What institutions does it use to "exclude"? None of it is mentioned, of course. Or rather, it is: it is spoken in the meritocratic language of individual responsibility. The excluder is the excluded. The excluded are those who do not adapt, who do not integrate. Those who can only blame themselves. It is valid for the white unemployed. It is even more valid for the indigenous unemployed who are supposed to be naturally/culturally (they are the same) unsuited to modern society. The SOS-Racism operation therefore inserted itself in the internal reclassifications of the white world, but the ideological reshaping to which it contributed on the left also participated in the offensive against Indigenous Power. The writings of indigenous militants often describe how SOS-Racisme "took over" the movement resulting from the March and "broke down" the autonomous organizations that appeared in its wake. This assertion should be put in perspective to the extent that this association was never able to take hold among immigrant populations except marginally. If SOS-Racisme "took over" anything, it was only the sympathy that the March had elicited from certain movements on the left and from white youth. The association founded by Julien Dray did not exclude immigrant and banlieue organizations from the political arena but from white media space and the white political field. Its *immediate* impact on youth organizations for those of colonial origins seems to me to have been limited but not negligible: SOS-Racisme "took over" potential white support (in particular some movements on the far left); it sowed problems among us and was able to "take over" a minority of us. It is not nothing, but, again, I think it is absurd to see SOS-Racisme as the primary cause of the failures of attempts at autonomous organization in the 1980s while at the same time asserting (correctly) its lack of an audience among immigrants and in neighborhoods. I tend to think that SOS-Racisme was in fact a weapon pointed at indigenous people but mainly *inside* the "white tribe," to borrow Wole Soyinka's expression.[97]

In March 1986, the first cohabitation government was formed under Jacques Chirac, and Charles Pasqua, the mentor who guided the first steps of the current head of state (Sarkozy), was the Interior Minister. He was determined to fight it out, consistent with the overall policy presented by Jacques Chirac to the National Assembly: "The Parliament will be debating a project to establish an administrative procedure to take foreigners in illegal situations to the border and a modification of the Code of Nationality aimed at subjecting the acquisition of French nationality to an act of prior intention. In terms of regulations, the government will reestablish visas for the arrival and residency of foreign nationals from outside the EEC."[98] A project that had the merit, so to speak, of providing a transparent expression of the different facets of the offensive against the indigenous, where the question of "illegals" acted as a fig leaf. Without revisiting the political consensus of 1984, the new Interior Minister turned to supplementing the repressive legislation on illegal immigration adopted by the former majority. He hardened its application and made multiple dramatic statements and actions to prove his dedication to the issue (sending home 101 Malians on a chartered plane). Above all, he had a new law passed establishing new, particularly restrictive conditions on the arrival and residency of non-community nationals (non-whites, to tell it as it is), heightened border checks, facilitated deportation, and extended the scope of application of "dual punishment," among other measures.

Following the presidential and legislative elections of 1988, the Left regained control of all the levers of power. It could not overlook the pressure from part of its voting base to repeal repressive laws. However, faced with the development of the white, working-class resistance that had expressed itself in the lightning-quick rise of the Front National (Le Pen received more than 14% of the vote in the presidential election), it chose to continue following the trail blazed by prior governments. The Pasqua Law was not repealed and its application only relaxed (the number of deportations fell in the months following the elections). In August 1989, a new law on foreign entry and residency was finally passed; it removed the harshest measures that applied to immigrants in an irregular situation but preserved the principle of hunting illegal immigrants and closed borders. It fell well beneath the promises made by the Socialists during the campaign. For the Right, however, it was still too lax on immigration. Its slogan was "*immigration zero.*" And it was once again Charles Pasqua who took charge of implementing this program following the victory of Jacques Chirac in the presidential elections of 1993. In less than nine months, four ordinary statutes were announced that made entry and residency conditions in France stricter, established new restrictions on family reunification, limited the rights of foreign students, heightened police and administrative measures aimed at controlling immigration, increased deportations, and authorized preventive identity checks by the police. The Constitution was also modified to restrict the benefits of the right to asylum. Jean-Louis Debré, who followed Pasqua as Interior Minister, continued in the same direction.

The Socialist Jean-Pierre Chevènement as well! In fact, after the 1997 legislative elections, a new period of cohabitation government occurred. This time the Right was in the presidential palace and the Left had the majority in National Assembly and was tasked with forming a government. Named Prime Minister by Jacques Chirac, Lionel Jospin designated Jean-Pierre Chevènement as Interior Minister. The left had sided with undocumented immigrants during the great struggle of 1996; it had promised to repeal the Pasqua and Debré laws; and many had placed their trust in them. They were wrong. Adopted in April 1998 by the Socialist majority ("bravely" the Communists abstained and the Greens did not take part in the vote), the Chevènement Law only marginally improved the arrangements made by the Right:

elimination of the lodging certificate, relative expansion of conditions for granting of residence permits, relaxing of the system for mixed marriages and family reunification. As for the announced regularization of undocumented immigrants, in the end, it only concerned a little more than half of those who asked for it. As usual, the PS tried to placate its anti-racist voters by means of a few concessions while serving as a relay for white working-class resistance; a balancing act that was made all the more difficult by the increasing radicalization of this resistance. As a result, Jospin failed miserably in the presidential elections of 2002; the Right and far-right went face to face in the second round of voting. Jacques Chirac was elected with more than 80% of the vote and Nicolas Sarkozy was named Interior Minister. Unsurprisingly, his first mission was to solve the immigration problem, once and for all. He did not need to be asked twice… We know the rest: new laws, decrees, memoranda, secret guidelines, every political, administrative, and law enforcement means was deployed to find and deport immigrants in illegal situations and to make residency untenable for immigrants and their descendants. I won't elaborate but I think it is important to emphasize that Sarkozy's immigration policies did not come out of the blue. And it is not specific to the Right, save in its "frankness." Starting in the early 1980s, when the Socialists were all-powerful and in charge of the state, a consensus gradually developed between the main white parties that connected the suppression of immigration with "integration" of the "*beurs*." This consensus forms what could be called the *first axis of the white offensive against the indigenous*.

The *second axis* of this offensive is the reform of the Nationality Code. While disagreements between the Left and the Right exist on this question as on others, it is possible to speak of a fundamental consensus. Coming back to the middle of the 1980s, more specifically the time of the first cohabitation government, Charles Pasqua doggedly pursued immigration, and Albin Chalandon was the Minister of Justice who had the task of sealing the Nationality Code to close the door of French nationality to the children of immigration. Until then, the children born in France of foreign parents had automatically received the French nationality. Afterwards, according to the proposal of the RPR group in the National Assembly, they had to make a declaration to obtain the privilege of becoming French. Not yet a naturalization request, but almost. A de facto negation of jus soli. A revolution from the perspective of the universalist republican tradition. The jus soli established by the first Nationality Code of 1889 was one of the most important pillars of the myth of the "citizen nation" on which the Republic was based. Quite evidently, the RPR leadership had gone too far. Chalandon's proposal raised an outcry. The situation was all the more delicate for the governing right in that its project for university reform had provoked strong student protests around the same time. Chirac had little choice. He retreated. The legislative process was interrupted. A commission of "elders" presided over by Marceau Long was established to define the contours of a new white consensus on nationality. In January 1987, the Chalandon project was buried. It was not until 1993 that the Right could pass a reform, one that was less restrictive than one proposed a few years earlier, but it opened a first breach in the jus soli.[99] During the election campaigns of 1995 and 1997, the Left pledged to revisit this law. It only did so partially. The Guigou law on nationality passed in March 1998, on the pretext of respecting the autonomous will of children born in France of foreign parents, allowed them to decline French nationality on reaching adulthood.[100] The reforms of the Nationality Code as envisaged by the Right only seemed to have the problem of being too audacious. Too frank for the Republic. The Socialist left favored calling the jus soli into question but only in concealed fashion, only if it were possible to present it as a new expression of the democratic and universalist aspects of the Republic.

The right was less careful. It was aware that jus soli was part of the republican dogma constitutive of "national identity" but this identity appeared threatened in another of its more important foundations: white-European-Christian privilege. Valéry Giscard d'Estaing, a man of the democratic liberal right, admitted it bluntly. In the conclusion to a column called "Immigration or Invasion?" in 1991, he admitted the need to return "to the traditional idea of acquisition of French nationality, the birth right."[101] Who are these immigrants who are not content with invading French soil, but also occupy French nationality? The answer: Muslims![102]

Everything can be found there. From the perspective of republican "national identity," being French and Muslim is an oxymoron. It is not possible to be both one and the other. At least as long as the idea of the nation, as it was constructed in the Republic, is not radically reshaped, as long as "national identity" connects "Gallic" privilege with white-European-Christian privilege. The offensive against Muslims—and against Islam, more generally[103]—represented one of the components of the defense of this two-fold privilege in the face of the indigenous specter. It is the *third axis* around which white consensus was built.

For Thomas Deltombe, who studies Islamophobia in the media, "the massive strikes in the automobile industry between 1982 and 1984 marked a decisive turn in the relationship between the government and immigrants: references to Islam would be used by the government to discredit a strike that had little to do with religion. When the OS strike began in the spring of 1982 in the Citroën and Talbot factories of Aulnay-sous-Bois and Poissy, the media turned quickly to the 'Islamic' aspects of this mobilization that the traditional union leaders were having trouble channeling. Company mosques […] suddenly flooded television screens. Photos of praying specialized workers were plastered throughout the print media. Caricaturists transformed factory chimneys into minarets. Rumors of 'fundamentalist' manipulation spread. The press on the extreme right, of course, let fly against the 'Khomeinist' workers. Gaston Deferre, the Socialist Interior Minister, spoke of 'the holy wars of fundamentalists, Muslims, and Shiites.' The next day, Prime Minister Pierre Mauroy declared: 'The main difficulties that remain are raised by immigrant workers, whose problems are not unknown to me but who, it is clear, are being agitated by religious and political groups that are motivated by criteria that have little to do with French social realities.'"[104]

The Islam front was opened; it became increasingly important to the strategy of White Power in that the new generations resulting from immigration were increasingly numerous in following the religion of their parents. In 1989, the Iranian fatwa against Salman Rushdie and then the first veil "affair" marked a new stage in the construction of white consensus, a consensus that became more widespread because it extended to a fringe of the far left. The primary beneficiary was the Front National. On November 26, 1989, it obtained record scores in the legislative by-elections of Dreux and Marseille. As soon as the results were published, the Socialist Prime Minister, Michel Rocard, declared that France could not "house all the misery of the world,"[105] followed by Mitterrand who stated that "the threshold of tolerance was reached in the 1970s."[106] Jacques Chirac, for his part, asserted that France had "a saturation problem."[107] He called for border closures, a greater crackdown on illegal immigration, reform of the right to asylum and the Nationality Code. Talking about Islam in France means talking about immigration!

From that point on, the offensive against Islam would continue to grow against the backdrop of international political upheavals and their sometimes deadly repercussions in France.[108] From 1993 to 1995, there was a second cohabitation government. Jacques Chirac was once again Prime Minister; Charles Pasqua returned to his position at the Interior Ministry on Place Beauvau. He spared no efforts in feeding the fear of Islam and justified his government's support for the Algerian military junta that, after "halting the electoral process" in 1992, had waged a veritable war against Islamist political organizations. The left shared this orientation in the name of defending secularity and women's liberation. It was also a good opportunity to reignite the old colonial division between the Kabyle and Arab peoples. The former were supposedly democratic, secular, and respectful of women's rights. Truly civilized. The latter were the opposite. In the fall of 1994, the Minister of National Education François Bayrou announced the prohibition on wearing the veil in public establishments. The Conseil d'État canceled the decision, but the polemic returned. Another future candidate for the presidency, Ségolène Royale, declared at the time on France 2: "I would like to remind you that people kill over wearing the veil in Algeria. I believe that we shouldn't conflate all external signs of religion. I also believe that we have to question the degree of freedom these young women have since, behind the veil, I think that there is a political movement of adults, Islamism, that is still seeking to subvert equal rights for girls."[109] In *The Wretched of the Earth*, Fanon had already mentioned this type of colonial discourse: "In other places, you hear day in and day out hateful remarks about veiled women, polygamy, and the Arab's alleged contempt for the female sex."[110]

In public debate, Islam, immigration, banlieues, and security are systematically associated. Thomas Deltombe highlights how the media "insists on the 'natural' attraction of youth in the banlieues to Islamist ideas."[111] In 1995, suspected of involvement in terrorist attacks, Khaled Kelkal was killed in cold blood by the police. In the eyes of the majority, he was glaring proof that young Muslims of the projects had an almost natural inclination to violence. "The main questions posed by the media," notes Deltombe, "consisted of asking whether the young man acted because he was an 'Islamist' or because he was from the 'banlieue.' For a month, Islam became a phenomenon of the banlieue and the banlieue became a quasi-Islamic phenomenon, of which Kelkal was the symbol."[112] I could continue to describe all the pretexts impudently used by white political forces, their intellectuals, and their media to resuscitate the most abject colonial representations—from the barbarian to be tortured to the savage to be civilized. In the secular Republic, few dare to make public reference to the memory of the crusades but indirectly, by half gestures, between words, the subliminal message was the same as the one announced clearly by George Bush: Christian civilization is threatened by Muslim hordes. This Islamophobic fervor, further kindled by the September 11, 2001 attacks and American neocolonialism, reached its peak in 2003 with the affair of sisters Alma and Lila Lévy,[113] the veil law,[114] and the sordid campaign against Tariq Ramadan. From far right to far left, the white front became tighter. Those who took the risk of departing from this white consensus, mainly from the radical left, were rare.

The Islamophobic offensive took various forms: repressive, ideological, but also *assimilationist*. As a colonial political tactic, assimilationism has two facets. It consists, as we can recall, of sowing concern in the minds of the colonized, diluting identities, and covering over statutory inequalities. It also consists of dividing the colonized, promoting elites and cops from within them charged with supervising and controlling them, in particular through specific examples of representation implanted in the institutional structures of White Power. While the first facet of this tactic takes the form of valorizing "moderate Islam," promoting "modernist" Muslims, "emancipated" Muslims, its second facet is both complementary and antagonistic; it was barely sketched out in the Giscard era and began to be seriously implemented by the Socialist Interior Minister Pierre Joxe, who established the short-lived Conseil de reflection sur l'islam en France (Corif, Advisory Council on Islam in France) in 1989. The desire to organize the Muslim religion under the auspices of the state would be pursued by all subsequent Ministers of the Interior. Charles Pasqua, Jean-Louis Debré, Jean-Pierre Chevènement and, finally, Nicolas Sarkozy, the cleverest of all, who was responsible for the CFCM that was able to bring together the main Muslim organizations under the patronage of the Interior Ministry. In exchange for their "loyalism," for the efforts they carried out to drain Islam of any spirit of rebellion, for their collaboration in the policy of surveillance of Muslim populations, especially in housing projects, these organizations received institutional legitimacy, some concessions aimed at facilitating cultural practices, and, of course, sharing between each other—not without tensions—the "market" of French Islam. Aziz Zemmouri and Vincent Geisser have shown how this policy took its inspiration from the management of colonial Islam,[115] the similarity of their underlying ideologies, and the goals they pursued. "From the first period of conquest," they write, "the colonial administration attempted to impose a 'Muslim clergy'—an expression used by some in the colonial administration—intended to serve the interests of France loyally."[116] The objective of the "bureaucratization" of "Muslim clerks," as they explain, was to ensure their support for colonial authorities "and especially to prevent any attempts at religious resistance." Then and now, establishing official representation of Islam under the guidance of the administration "had as its logical counterpart a policy of surveillance and repression of so-called 'independent' religious figures, whose activities were deemed subversive." The organization of an institutionalized representation of Islam came with the intention to develop official structures for training "tailor-made imams" and stifling associations that tried to encourage the spread of an independent Islam. The government's policy in this regard was communicated by intermediary state authorities, local towns and municipalities, the primary mediators of white working-class resistance in neighborhoods that, often based on reports provided by the Intelligence Services, "practiced a form of favoritism towards certain Muslim associations reputed to be 'moderate' and 'presentable' to the detriment of other 'less respectable' associations that were conveniently labelled 'fundamentalist' and/or '*intégriste.*' The cases of cities like Montpellier, Marseille, or Vénissieux are prime examples of this authoritarian management where mayors tended to promote a loyal and faithful 'municipal Islam' while ostracizing all the other Muslim organizations at the same time."[117]

It would be wrong, however, to only see contemporary Islamophobia as the belated flatulence of an old Christian fear of "triumphant Islam." Its stench is the same but fermenting in the bowels of

Islamophobes is not hatred of Islam as a belief. It is much more the product of Islamophobic policy than the impetus behind it. It is less a question of defending or spreading Christianity for its own sake than consecrating its memory as one of the components of whiteness. The Islamophobes who tell us their only enemy is "radical Islam" are therefore only half-hypocrites. They are not defending Christianity against Islam; they are defending white superiority in its relatively secularized form today. "Radical Islam," from the perspective of these republicans is simply the intractable Islam that is reticent to Westernization, the Islam that is a crucible of indigenous dissidence. They see Muslims who want to express their Islamness in public spaces as radical Islamists not because they call secularity into question but because they encourage the indigenous to assert themselves in the public arena. They are terrorists not because they kill "innocent victims" but at soon as they break into public space. It matters little to them whether Tariq Ramadan was in favor of stoning; in their eyes, he was a "fundamentalist," he had ties with "terrorism," because he told Muslims: don't stay away from public space, engage in politics. When Islamophobes denounce "Muslim proselytism," they are talking less about religious proselytism than the incitement to occupy public space. When they prohibit veils in school, they are denying access to public space to the indigenous who object to being "*beur*-ified." When they claim to defend the emancipation of Muslim women while respecting their faith, it is another ploy: in fact, they want to prevent their emancipation *as indigenous*. Muslims, and the indigenous more broadly, are only welcome in public space on the strict condition that they take their frustration out on other Muslims, in other words that they fight among themselves. The Republic is an Islamophobic religion. Islamophobia does not fight Muslims as Muslims but Muslims as potential rebels against white order—and that's why every Muslim is a potential fundamentalist or terrorist. It does not develop primarily in the field of religious intolerance but in racial struggle. It is therefore only one aspect of this colonial counter-offensive against all indigenous, and more specifically against the preferred place of their resistance, the working-class housing projects where the different facets of security policy come together.

Security policy represents the *fourth axis* around which white consensus is formed. Connecting participation in the machinery of the war on "Islamic terrorism" on an international scale, repression of so-called radical Islam in France, securing European and French borders against illegal migration, structures to fight clandestine immigration within metropolitan France, police selection, surveillance, and pressure against legal immigration, expansion, consolidation, diversification, rationalization, and modernization of the police tools and judicial procedures destined to fight "insecurity" in working-class neighborhoods, the soft left and hard right have produced a vast war machine with multiple ramifications in every sphere of social life. One of its main objectives is to counter Indigenous Political Power. France did not have its own Twin Towers; it had the Levy sisters. It did not have Kabul; it had Clichy-sous-Bois. It did not have a "new Hitler"; it had "riffraff (*racailles*)." It did not have "Desert Storm"; it had a colonial curfew. It did not have its democratic "Greater Middle East"; it had its "Banlieue Plan." It did not have Jalal Talabani; it had Fadela Amara. It did not have its "marines"; it had its BAC (anti-crime brigade). It did not have Bush; it had Sarkozy. However, Sarkozy's policy to subdue neighborhoods reaches back far into the past.

The theme of juvenile delinquency among the inhabitants of these neighborhoods appeared at the turn of the 1970s and 1980s, in particular after the 1981 riots. The question of "insecurity" gradually became a major electoral issue. It structured the polemics during the campaign for the municipal elections in 1983, the legislative elections in 1986, and now resurfaces at each election.

Apparently aimed at responding to the growing concerns of the French in the face of "incivility" and "urban violence," it modeled this concern and contributed to spreading and radicalizing white working-class resistance. The consensus between the traditional right and the government on the left only occurred slowly in terms of the forms of coercion and control to impose on the inhabitants of housing projects. The turning point was the indigenous resistance expressed in the form of the Vaulx-en-Velin revolts in the banlieue of Lyon in October 1990 and then in the Parisian banlieues of Sartrouville, Mantes-la-Jolie, Meaux, and Garges-lès-Gonesse between March and July 1991. The Socialists also reacted to white working-class pressure. In 1995, Gérard Le Gall, one of the "experts" of the Socialist Party responsible for analyzing shifts in public opinion, wrote several reports for party leaders on the need to "harden" their discourse on "immigration and insecurity" to "win back" the votes of the "working-class."[118] His proposals were heeded in June 1997 when Lionel Jospin, Prime Minister of the third cohabitation at the time, announced that "security" would be the "second priority" of his government, the first being unemployment. A few months later, at the PS congress in Villepinte, he repeated it. As usual, the racist strategy draped itself in the mantle of the Enlightenment: "Security is a value of the Left," the Prime Minister was not afraid to assert; it is inscribed in the "right to safety" in the Declaration of Human Rights.[119] The threshold was crossed: right and left now shared the same concept of security. Only minor divergences would remain, sometimes artificially inflated to win votes. Shortly after the destruction of the Twin Towers, the Socialist Daniel Vaillant, who followed Chevènement at the Interior Ministry, concocted the loi sur la Sécurité quotidienne (LSQ, Law on Everyday Security) that was passed almost unanimously by Parliament.[120] Officially designed to be a weapon against terrorism, it also contained repressive measures against the inhabitants of housing projects. It was responsible in particular for prohibiting gatherings in staircases! Right and left rivaled in their ardor to convince their voters that they were the best ones to ensure their safety. In its previously mentioned "Column," the LMSI group revealed that the "themes of 'violence' and 'insecurity' were the themes most mentioned by the five main candidates: Jacques Chirac, Lionel Jospin, François Bayrou, Jean-Pierre Chevènement, and Jean-Marie Le Pen." Just as it had won the municipal elections soon after September 11, 2001, the Right displayed more homogeneity on this question and won the 2002 presidential election. To explain the defeat of its candidate as early as the first round of voting, the PS blamed the plurality of candidates on the left. The explanation lies elsewhere. Many likely PS voters, primarily concerned with the real or potential decline in their economic conditions, abstained or voted for candidates on the far left to express their defiance of the Socialists who were turning towards neoliberalism. Other voters, rallying around "insecurity," immigration, and Islam, placed their trust in the candidates that seemed the most determined. The 2002 presidential elections therefore represented the first major election in which a racial vote demonstrated itself capable of shifting the political relationship of forces.

As soon as they took office, the new majority on the right already began preparing the next election. In the fall of 2002, the first Perben Law was passed on "the delinquency of minors" that strengthened the security measures implemented by the Socialists. In the winter of 2004, its repressive aspect was further heightened by the law on "organized criminality" called "Perben II." Nicolas Sarkozy, for his part, already had the ambition to become a candidate for the presidency. Named Interior Minister, he organized his main strategy around intensifying social race struggles, hoping—correctly—to seduce Front National voters. The symbolic security of whites was necessarily his priority. And to ensure the security of whites, it is naturally necessary to terrorize non-whites. I mentioned above the different aspects of the strategy he employed, in particular in terms of immigration. However, the main area where white resistance collided with indigenous resistance was the working-class housing projects. As a result, the bulk of the Interior Minister's efforts were directed there, with explicit support from the Socialists Julien Dray and Daniel Vaillant. Wherever indigenous were present, repression intensified, police presence was reinforced, surveillance increased, and the arsenal available to the various police forces was "militarized." In the "sensitive neighborhoods," a permanent state of exception was established. Yet Sarkozy was a shrewd operator. He may have also been poorly "integrated." Or more "white cosmopolitan," like his corporate friends, than nationalist in the manner of de Gaulle. He was first and foremost a statesman; he belonged to the state and defended its interests. Whatever the case, he showed himself to be more flexible with republican dogma than other political leaders, not hesitating to promote "positive discrimination" and recommending the promotion of elites from housing projects and immigration, presaging the nomination of indigenous ministers and the Banlieue Plan. In addition, at the risk of being accused of "communitarianism," he sought to reconcile with Muslims to take votes from the Socialists, towards whom the majority of voters issuing from immigration generally tended. The CFCM was also there for that. For his part, the Minister of Housing, Jean-Louis Borloo, led the offensive on another level, cleaning the banlieues, dispersing the indigenous in urban space, and relegating the most unlucky of them to the periphery of cities in the name of "social mixing" and "urban revitalization." The institutional left, whose strength resides in the network of municipalities controlled by its elected officials, did not oppose it. It had been behind the City Policy and various urban planning measures that strongly contributed to shriveling the populations of the banlieue and exacerbating racial differentiation. I will return to this point in more detail in the following chapter. Suffice it to say that urban policy is the *fifth axis* underlying white consensus.

If there were any further doubts about the meaning of the policy implemented by the main authorities of the French state, it is enough to mention the ideological campaign aimed at rekindling the colonial dimension of the "national identity." The rehabilitation of colonization represents the *sixth axis* on which white consensus is built. What difference is there, in fact, between Sarkozy declaring in Dakar that "the drama of Africa is that African man has not sufficiently entered history" and Chevènement stating: "colonization is also the moment when the African continent was drawn into the dynamic of Universal History"?[121] Started in the early 1990s, this offensive was, unsurprisingly, deployed more extensively after the September 11, 2001 attacks and flourished again after the November 2005 revolts. The first major moment was the famous law of February 23, 2005 that aimed to reintroduce the "good work" France did in the colonies into the school curriculum.[122] The most problematic paragraphs of this law were finally retracted following the protests of several intellectuals and associations but the rehabilitation of colonialism in other forms—speeches by political leaders, publication of articles and works, delocalized initiatives on the municipal level (commemorations, museums, etc.)—became one of the main concerns of White Power, vaguely cloaked by the desire to separate the most violent methods of colonial expansion from the republican truth that was necessarily beneficial to the colonized. Every immigrant or child of immigrants carries colonization inside them. And colonization carries in itself the condemnation of the Republic. Political and *moral* condemnation. "Repentance" is not decolonization. Not for the Republic and not for the immigrant. It only *appears* to close a history: "Come on, I said sorry and let's speak of it no more!" It closes and opens. Repentance requires more. Forgiveness cannot be reconciled with recidivism. And the Republic lives on repeat offences. Blacks, Arabs, and Muslims are always indigenous. The identity of the Republic is colonization, in other words, racial hierarchy. When Sarkozy associates immigration, national identity, and denunciation of repentance, he is denouncing the Republic. He is like an informant. There is always a grain of truth in the words of our adversaries. Colonization is also slavery. And talking about slavery means talking about the responsibility of the French state. It does not matter if it is from the monarchy or the Napoleonic Empire, the revisionist Republic doesn't want to hear about it. The entire "history of France" is sacred. Even that bungler Clovis is sacred. Attacking it would mean attacking the "national identity." Under pressure from protests in the Antilles, parliamentarians even consented to adopt the Taubira draft law[123] but they first emptied it of its substance. The slave trade and slavery were certainly recognized as "crimes against humanity" but France did not have any particular responsibility; the article on reparations was cast aside; the commitments made on the teaching of slavery in school were quickly forgotten. In 2006, following a speech by President Chirac, the date of May 10 was reserved to "honor the memory of slaves and commemorate the abolition of slavery." It was above all a way to honor the Republic that abolished slavery in 1848, but it was also a small progress, a reflection of Antillean struggles and the policies aimed at neutralizing them. On this question, as on others, a consensus was established between the different factions of White Power. Behind the question of slavery, there was another issue: preventing the connection between the struggles of the Antilleans and those of the descendants of Maghreb immigrants living in the same neighborhoods. As such, white publicists endeavored to dissociate slavery from the colonization of Africa and the Americas. European and French responsibility was blended into the vague denunciation of a slavery that all civilizations would have practiced and, *more specifically…* Arab-Muslim civilization! Dehistoricized, the recognition of slavery as a crime against humanity lost all its ethical and, especially, political dimensions. It simply became an expression of the values of humanism and, more precisely, a new profession of faith in the "spirit of the Enlightenment," the standards of Western modernity; while the intention grew to oppose the bad, lazy, thieving, deceitful, violent, and dreadful slave-owning Arab with the good, peaceful, docile, and hard-working Negro. The maneuver, however, is even more complex. White Power also endeavored to feed another line of separation: opposing the wild Negro of Africa, the illegal border-crosser, Muslim, and polygamist, great grandson of a slave owning tribe with the domestic Negro of the Antilles, French for four centuries and proud of it, enhanced by a few drops of white blood in the veins, frequent churchgoer, lover of France and the Republic, and attentive to "sharing its painful memory." I am using the most hackneyed stereotypes that go back to slavery and colonization on purpose. For even though, for the most part, they are only rarely used so crudely, it only takes a little attention to the discourse of many political leaders, intellectuals, and other journalists to discover the worst colonial representations.

The racialist aspect of the policies aimed at fragmenting the indigenous that come from different colonial histories does not only come from their end goal, preserving white supremacy, it is already contained in the ideology that feeds them.

7

Working-Class Neighborhoods: The Epicenter of the Struggle of the Social Races

"You can get into a conversation with a person, and in five minutes tell whether or not that person's scope is broad or whether that person's scope is narrow, whether that person is interested in things going on in his block where he lives or interested in things going on all over the world. Now persons who are narrow-minded, because their knowledge is limited, think that they're affected only by things happening in their block. But when you find a person who has a knowledge of things of the world today, he realizes that what happens in South Vietnam can affect him if he's living on St. Nicholas Avenue, or what's happening in the Congo affects his situation on Eighth Avenue or Seventh Avenue or Lenox Avenue. The person who realizes the effect that things all over the world have right on his block, on his salary, on his reception or lack of reception into society, immediately becomes interested in things international. But if a person's scope is so limited that he

thinks things that affect him are only those things
that take place across the street or downtown, then
he's only interested in things across the street and
downtown."

—Malcolm X, 1965

There are clear reasons why the main targets of the colonial counter-revolution are the working-class housing projects. First, these neighborhoods are a place of great social and political vulnerability, places that can be legitimately attacked because they were historically reserved for the lower classes; and, simply, because they are peripheral and therefore not entirely from here, distant, and everything that is distant is *a priori* "savage." These neighborhoods are in particular places where there is a concentration of immigrants and their children. Independently of their real social composition, they are seen as ghettos of immigrants or children of immigrants, a threat to "national cohesion" and white supremacy. Yet while the danger is largely overestimated, it is no less real. Because *the heart of Indigenous Power is indeed found in working-class neighborhoods.*

Places of life and not mere lodgings, places of memory where ties of all sort are made, working-class housing projects are in fact the privileged space of a social power that, far from being inorganic and vain, is slowly transforming into political power: the power of multiform resistance, the power of cultural creation/subversion, the power to influence political decisions starting with local institutions, the power of organization as networks, communities, associations, families, mosques and other places of worship, and the power to defragment different segments of immigration and construct relations of mutual aid and solidarity, including with certain sectors of the white population. And this power must be kept from consolidating, neutralized, broken, turned against itself.

However, these neighborhoods are also one of the main spaces in which white resistance is deployed. In wealthy neighborhoods, that are not called "neighborhoods" (*quartiers*), it is at the same time all-powerful, blindingly evident—simply because few indigenous people are seen there save for the helpful, smiling "Arab at the corner grocery"—and invisible, for that same reason.[124] White resistance benefits in fact from the economic and political power of the inhabitants of these neighborhoods as the dominant class. Rich ghettos are protected from the mass intrusion of indigenous people because of the high price of houses, while the municipalities that manage them refuse to accept the public housing quotas to which they are legally bound. A very different situation from that of working-class neighborhoods. Socially and politically dominated in a white world, the whites of working-class neighborhoods are in a less favorable power relation in the face of the omnipresent indigenous. Or more precisely, in different ways depending on the segments, generations, and places of residence, they have contradictory relationships with the indigenous. Statutory resistance in the neighborhoods is first due to the white "middle classes" and working aristocracy, frightened by the possibility of symbolic downgrading. It is also due to some sectors of the most destitute levels of the white population. Often, although not without a certain solidarity or relationships of complicity with indigenous at the professional or micro-local level, the white working classes are brought to react negatively (and even *very* negatively) to the indigenization of their neighborhoods or to what they perceive as a barbarian "invasion" of France. They do not always engage in white racial resistance by the political choices made in one election or another, for example; it is often through microscopic, invisible social practices that they do not necessarily understand. This resistance can take the form of just an unkind word, insult, or humiliation, or, more seriously, harassment, physical aggression, or even murder. It occurs through various mediations that often mask the racial logic, like the flight from public housing, bypassing the school map (before its removal by the current Minister of Education), demands to strengthen security policies, pressure to prevent the construction of a mosque, or pushing municipal authorities to establish "quotas" and other "tolerance thresholds." It manifests itself directly by practices of racial discrimination performed by individuals who have some power of administrative or economic decision. But it also expresses itself cruelly, unapologetically, in firm support for the parties leading the offensive against immigration and the populations emerging from it.

Along with the police and judicial authorities that can easily be pointed out, multiple public or private institutions relay this white resistance. The municipal institutions that redesign or renovate their towns to attract "whites" and put off indigenous people, heighten controls, surveillance, repression, establish curfews, prohibit the participation of non-whites in decision-making structures, hold rigorous aid and grant selection processes for indigenous associations, and manipulate community solidarity; prefectural authorities that resign in the face of demands from various public housing organizations establishing "quotas"; middle school leaders who allow bypassing the school map or adopt measures aimed at increasing their attractiveness, contributing to aggravating social and racial distinctions; organizations that provide jobs, internships, temporary work that expresses the discriminatory demands of employers—no matter if it is reluctantly; and others. A thousand printed pages in small font probably would not be enough to list all the practices—voluntary or involuntary, direct or indirect, determined by a sort of culturalist paternalism, by openly racist representations or management imperatives, whether they are destined to cozy up to their constituency or motivated by the desire to "unite the Left to block the Right"—all the practices that reproduce racial hierarchies on a local scale paralyze indigenous resistance and respond to the demands for "ethnic cleansing," or frankly encourage them.

As long it does not risk causing too much "social disorder" or revealing the racial reality of the Republic, the entire institutional architecture at the local, regional, departmental, and national levels transmits and encourages white resistance. However, the main driver is at the head of the state and in the leadership of the most powerful parties.

There is little doubt that the disastrous social consequences of neoliberal policies have considerably worsened working-class racism. Or rather, I would tend to say, they have contributed to making the *defense of white privilege* (and more generally national privilege) a decisive factor in mobilizing the white working class. Nevertheless, the socioeconomic situation and the decline of the organized labor movement are not enough to explain this evolution. It can be seen in the *consistency* of this racial working-class resistance *beyond speculation* and in the importance of the stakes represented, for the French Communist Party, by the struggle against the presence of immigrants in the "red banlieues." For me, it is important to grasp the particularly perverse aspect of the sociopolitical calculations that occur in neighborhoods, the local resonance of the intertwined social, national, and racial dimensions of the republican pact.

First, we need to take a step back. More precisely to the period between the 1960s and 1970s influenced by the power of the labor movement, including the urban fabric. The social state was still a reality, even if was starting to show timid steps towards disengagement, notably in terms of public housing. Colonization and the trauma of decolonization were less than ten years prior. The number of immigrants from the colonies was undergoing a new surge. The heritage of colonialization was still direct and transparent in the ways this immigration was handled, in companies and housing as well as in its political and administrative treatment. And, of course, in the dominant representations. We were at the time in a political and economic context that was much different than the current reality. However, in working-class neighborhoods, white resistance was already very real. It was mainly led by the PCF (French Communist Party), the same PCF whose strength in the first half of the twentieth century came in part from its ability to integrate European immigrants,[125] but which then decided to defend white workers to the detriment of immigrant workers from the colonies. After World War II and up to the 1970s, the "red banlieues" were proud of being what they were, the territory where social struggles unfolded, where the gains from these struggles were inscribed in the living spaces and residences of the working class. In the large plants, skilled workers mixed with the more fortunate salaried workers (employees, technicians…) who were the main support for communist municipalities. The urban renovation projects that they promoted seemed to guarantee workers at the time access to an urban environment and "modern" housing standards reflecting a social and cultural mobility that brought them closer to the housing conditions and ways of life of the middle class. The ambition of the proletariat is to resemble the petit bourgeoisie. And the ambition of proletarian cities was to resemble petit bourgeois cities. The city as a whole wanted its standard of living to progress; it wanted to change its status, increase its dignity. The red banlieues tended to remain white banlieues.

Under these circumstances, the aggravation of Communist elected officials in the face of an influx of immigrants (especially Algerians and Moroccans at the time) into their towns was not surprising, since the presence of immigrants would lower the social and symbolic value of their city. They were not only Arabs but, moreover, condemned to be part of the lower levels of the working class that held little interest for the PCF and its union branch, the CGT. I wrote "aggravation" to be polite. In fact, I should have said: they were outraged! All these miserable towelheads, living as they please, pulling the city down! And there was even less reason to accommodate them because they cost a lot of money.[126] In addition, you can't expect any votes from them because they don't have the right to vote! That is what Communist officials thought before shutting the door in the face of an immigrant household seeking to be rehoused in a public housing project. In the early 1960s,[127] as conveyed by the PCF, white resistance already expressed itself in the desire to distance and distribute in urban space all those whose overly visible presence would sully the city. At the end of the decade and in subsequent years, as the government increased the number of decisions aimed at making left-leaning municipalities bear the financial weight of public housing and the cost of receiving foreigners,[128] communist officials were obsessed with the immigration question, and more specifically the question of the indigenous. These elected officials led a campaign to oppose the residency of immigrants in their towns and called for them to be dispersed. Although they did not use the term, they called for "national preference" in 1969: "At a time when hundreds of thousands of French families are waiting for housing, financing the rehousing of immigrant workers cannot and must not in any case be placed on local budgets."[129] The symbolic, political, and budgetary burden that immigrants represented was one of the stakes of the struggle between a government on the right and Communist elected officials, between red cities and bourgeois cities. It is true that PCF leaders saw immigrants as a millstone that the Right was trying to throw around their necks. And the white proletariat fought against it.

Under the cover of social pretexts, "anti-racist" alibis, or in the name of "defending immigrant workers against slumlords," who were often immigrants themselves, the Communists wanted to purge their cities of the "*surplus*" of indigenous people. A pamphlet distributed in Gennevilliers in 1973 leaves little doubt about the desire to mobilize the "*good French*" against immigration: "We call for the population as a whole to support the action of the city council to stop and then reduce the percentage of immigration to our city."[130] The

PCF gradually adopted less explicit language but hardly changed its policy in the subsequent decades. It would lose its main urban bastions, but its successors on the right or from the PS, who competed in efforts to undermine the "working-class consciousness" and disrupt spaces of resistance, also became the spokespeople of the white working class panicked by its social and statutory down-grading exacerbated by economic upheaval and changes to the political field. With the disintegration of the independent political power of the working class and the organs that represented it, at stake was not only the dismantling of social gains but also their *status as citizens*. Social citizenship in the company, "urban" citizenship rooted in cities, political citizenship through parliamentary representation, workers slowly lost most of the mediations that they had acquired and that allowed them to not be a mere "labor force" but more than that: an independent political body, nation in the nation, *future* of the nation. Universal suffrage itself lost its meaning. In other terms, two things crumbled with the end of the welfare state and the unraveling of a citizenship mediated both by the state and the institutions of the working class itself: on one side, their integration in the national-state and, on the other, their dignity as a community of workers. Nationality was emptied of all social and civil content except in terms of those who were not national or seen as such; it no longer had or it tended to no longer have as its only dimension "Frenchness," the unstable mix of historical myths concocted by the Third Republic and a firm belief in European, Christian, and white superiority. De-citizenized nationality then showed its racial core; "*whiteness*" was the last privilege granted by the Republic to the white working classes. And this privilege of being "*good French*" and "*good whites*" absolutely had to be protected from the indigenous hordes taking over France.

This issue became more crucial in the peripheral urban areas in that escaping them increasingly became an impossible dream. Poverty, unemployment, insecurity, and a general rise in rent and housing prices prevented many inhabitants of working-class neighborhoods, including the upper levels of the working class, from having any hopes of finding new lodging or acquiring property in wealthier residential areas. In addition: sectors that previously had the means to reject public housing were now forced to turn to it. Aggravating the internal differences of the world of labor and the internal differences of the social housing stock resulting in particular from the state's gradual disengagement and the adoption of managerial norms for public housing management contributed to confining the most vulnerable layers of the white proletariat in the most disadvantaged urban segments characterized by an increasingly massive presence of immigrants.[131] Escape no longer being possible, the white proletariat could only doggedly defend the superiority of its status.

Olivier Masclet has published a long, very revelatory work analyzing the urban processes through which some layers of the working classes engage in white resistance. I am tempted to cite a long passage: "The possibility that some French households leave these buildings in the case where their "*Arab aspect*" might increase is only one aspect of the pressure placed on the representatives of the Office. It is also and especially manifested in the electoral field. The Lénine and Diderot buildings were the ones in Gennevilliers that gave the most votes to the Front National (with the joint ownership property buildings). These voters were not only lost for municipal elections, they were also spokespeople for the "security cause" that gradually imposed itself on all tenants. Forced to live in proximity to buildings inhabited by immigrant families, feeling threatened by young people "hanging out" outside their homes, the French tenants of municipal buildings constantly report their fear and resentment. Maintaining French households with average incomes and sorting tenants in fact had the result of increasing the feeling of vulnerability, even repressive measures by the captive French. The coming together of retired persons, single women, poor working-class households, and French with average incomes who were not able to follow the collective trajectory of leaving the HLM led to coalizing into a single expression of rejection of Arabs the resentment caused by ageing, lack of job security, family destitution, the rise in consumer norms in terms of lodging, and solitude. Like a 'perverse effect,' this hardening of opinions was the result of a policy of selecting households that aims to preserve the social value of the neighborhood. It required the municipality to transform these buildings into veritable 'bunkers' to protect their occupants from 'risks' in the environment."[132]

And by "environment," we understand that it means indigenous people!

The white working classes therefore experience the presence of immigrants in their "environment" as a downgrade in status, one that is all the harder to experience in that they made many sacrifices in the vain hope of resembling the middle class. Olivier Masclet also notes that "the inhabitants [of the neighborhoods] who feel both socially relegated, territorially dispossessed, and threatened in their future are prone to compensating their downgrading by giving value to the fact that they are French."[133] However, as Abdelmalek Sayad indicates, the fact that many immigrants and their children are now French somewhat depreciates the French nationality.

It becomes a "discount"[134] nationality. To defend their symbolic status, the *souchiens* ("original French") are obliged to defend the "quality" of French nationality: being "real French" would now mean being of white, European, and Christian origin. White proletarians are not part of the dominant class but are part of the dominant community. A far from negligible advantage.

In this case, white popular resistance appears to be a *perverse effect* of class struggle. The famous "social diversity" that figures at the center of the racial offensive against Indigenous Power is also, as Sylvie Tissot writes, "the poor weapon of poor towns." It represents "one of the rare tools left at the disposal of these cities when their wealthier neighbors can close their territory quite effectively to 'undesirable' populations without public assistance structures, even bypassing them when necessary."[135] Defending their status as white is also, in this particular context, a form of *proletarian struggle* against the decline caused by employer and neoliberal policies; it is both an *antagonistic* and *complementary* form of white bourgeois resistance that is useless but nonetheless real. It seems particularly simplistic or even naïve to speak of "articulation" between anti-racist or decolonial struggle and the struggle of the working classes without accounting for the fact that the latter are already connecting themselves to the struggle of white status. This dual condition—socially dominated and dominant in status—makes the white working classes both a mediation of and a large stake in the strategy of White Power. It is not simply a question of "dividing" the working class or turning French workers against the "scapegoat" of immigrants. Even more, as the dismantlement of the social state progresses and as French nationalism coincides less and less with the interests of the dominant classes, it was a question of *uniting* whites beyond their social oppositions in a republican pact recomposed around its racial dimension.

The category of "sensitive neighborhoods" that asserts and contributes to producing *the territorialization of social ruptures, represents a privileged component of this strategy*. Working-class neighborhoods are, in fact, the translation into space of political power relations. "The colonist's sector is a sector built to last, all stone and steel. It's a sector of lights and paved roads, where the trash cans constantly overflow with strange and wonderful garbage, undreamed-of leftovers. […] The colonist's sector is a white folks' sector, a sector of foreigners. The colonized's sector, or at least the 'native' quarters, the shanty town, the Medina, the reservation, is a disreputable place inhabited by disreputable people. You are born anywhere, anyhow. You die anywhere, from anything. It's a world with no space, people are piled one on top of the other […]. The colonized's sector is a famished sector, hungry for bread, meat, shoes, coal, and light. The colonized's sector is a sector that crouches and cowers, a sector on its knees, a sector that is prostrate. It's a sector of niggers, a sector of towel-heads."[136] The author of *The Wretched of the Earth* is not describing a territorial break but the transposition of the colonial break in the urban configuration. In the same way that in the glorious era of the "red banlieues" the struggles waged from and within these territories represented a spatial extension of class struggle at the level of companies, a moment of class struggle, today, the struggles waged in neighborhoods should not be understood as tied to essentially urban problems but as the spatial framework of a global racial struggle. This does not mean that the "imagined communities" on the level of cities are simply imaginary. They are both imaginary and real. "Neighborhoodism," which is one of its political figures, is not only the reflection of a false consciousness but also the expression of knowledge of a very real reality: the reality of the distribution and hierarchization of populations in differentiated residential spaces. Neighborhoodism does not see that these hierarchies include the materialization of sociopolitical conflicts in urban processes, conflicts that find their logic *outside* neighborhoods. Neighborhoodism therefore appears like the twin brother of the narrowest trade unionism that confines class struggle to the confines of the company.

Much more than the previous generation, white generations born starting in the 1980s were deeply affected by the effects of liberal restructuring and by the full-throttle offensive against working-class neighborhoods. Their historical trajectories and their careers determine other tropisms than those of their ancestors. Rooted in the same social conditions, the same feeling of relegation, the same institutional control, in particular by the police, the same exteriority in relation to the political field and decision-making mechanisms, a common consciousness and powerful solidarities are built between young whites—or those that economic insecurity keeps in a lasting social in-between—and the indigenous. Together, they are also subject to the old stereotypes associated with the "dangerous classes" of the nineteenth century that were so analogous to the racial representations of the "savage" of the colonies. And while the indigenous are stigmatized, additionally, for being indigenous, the young whites of the housing projects suffer from their social, cultural, affinity proximity to the actual "savages," the descendants of the colonized with whom they are often assimilated. Their privileges as French and white are *relatively* diminished in the face of what could be called a *tendency* to indigenization. Blacks rub off on the whites—I could have said Arabs or Muslims, of course.

In varying degrees, this phenomenon of *trend-based, partial* indigenization, *differentiated* according to spaces and populations affects many working-class neighborhoods through the effects of globalization, distribution, and contagion, independently of the effective mass of indigenous that live there. Indigenization is a drop of oil that spreads in the weave of the peripheral urban fabric as new generations of whites fall into the "sub-proletariat," into insecurity and distress. These young whites, who are already ostracized as "excluded," are now ostracized as semi-indigenous. We could call them politically mixed-race. They are refused employment, housing, and leisure; the police hound them; justice disdains them; teachers are afraid of them; not only because they belong to the lower classes but also, in an increasing way, because they are identified with their real or virtual next-door neighbors who have darker skin and strange customs. As in some of the current colonies, the indigenous *by assimilation* can have white skin and be the descendant of a Gaul. This movement of relative indigenization *tends* to widen the colonial fracture on a national scale. When White Power *fabricates* what it calls the "*lost territories of the Republic*," when it carves out insecure areas in space, when it distinguishes "*at-risk*" populations, when it opposes "*the France that is afraid*" and "*sensitive neighborhoods*" that are too indigenous for its taste, it is *producing* at the same time a "territorial" fracture that includes some of the colonial fracture. Resistance in working-class neighborhoods to structures that increase "territorial" or social inequalities then takes on an undeniably decolonial dimension. The political power of whites rebelling against the indigenous condition that, *in part*, oppresses them like it does nonwhites itself becomes, also *in part*, a moment of Indigenous Political Power.

I need to add some nuance again, some clarification. I am describing a tendency, a process that does not develop linearly or without contradictions. The reality of neighborhoods is particularly heterogeneous and the ways they connect to social and political space are very different. Especially when the colonial fracture by the rampant indigenization of working-class neighborhoods takes both the real and apparent form of a territorial fracture, it has the paradoxical result of blurring racial divides and masking the privileges—albeit very relative privileges—held by the young whites in the housing projects. The struggle of social races does not immediately appear as such. It does in the minds of those who hold power and know what to expect! But in the consciousness of the "banlieue youth," it does not appear as such. The solidarities woven above and beyond origins and nationalities, the emergence of a neighborhood culture, shared resistance, the weight of republican ideology crystallized in public institutions and policies strengthen the illusory sense, even among the indigenous, that nothing distinguishes a white unemployed youth from an indigenous unemployed youth. The CRS Flash-Ball—a "*less-lethal or sublethal hand-held weapon*" to use the manufacturer's words—seems to make no distinction between whites and indigenous.

Racial reality, however, is more stubborn than the concrete of housing projects. Even when it is minimal or occasional, the indigenous remain subject to special treatment and specific discrimination even when they are French. When white people are subjected to similar treatment, they at least have the symbolic privilege of being French and white. And they know it. And they can potentially use it. The multiple systems for marking, relegation, control, and repression, even when they reduce them in part to the condition of the indigenous, even when they are nourished by the colonial memory of bureaucratic and police institutions of the Republic, do not remove their privilege as white French. The "integration" of whites into indigenousness is just as impossible as the "integration" of the indigenous into the Republic.

And for the same reasons. A white person converted to Islam can "deconvert." An Arab, even a completely atheistic one, remains a Muslim. The Algerian Harkis who did so much—and so often—to blend into the anonymous masses of the "People of France" learned it at their expense. Blacks and Arabs are definitively on the other side of the racial barrier in the order of the Republic. They carry this barrier in their body, in their histories, in their daily lives. Not only because France has told it to them, in the past and present; because they fight them *in particular* for what they are supposed to have *in particular*. But because they also inherited a memory, a culture transmitted for better or worse by the indigenous generations that preceded them and that the Republic and Eurocentrism endeavor to deny, stifle, and disqualify; because they also inherited the ruptures of colonization, emigration, and rejection, hardened, sedimented, made lasting by their continued existence as indigenous; because finally they kept in themselves the traces of individual resistance, of collective struggle, and of the preserved pride of the indigenous in the face of the state of indignity to which some wanted to reduce them.

In his works, Frantz Fanon shed light on the violence inherent in colonial relationships. Abdelmalek Sayad, in a different but very similar register, continued this work wielding the scalpel of *partial* sociology. He revealed the colonialism-neocolonialism dialectic inscribed in the flesh and bones of the "emigrant-immigrant"; he dissected the mechanisms of permanent indigenization produced by the state and "state thinking"; more than anyone, he plumbed the "soul" of the indigenous in France, their children and the children of their children; he cracked forbidden safes, he revealed to those who did not want to know or talk about the painful intertwining of colonial humiliations, the pride regained after independence, the devastating and shameful wrenching from the soil, from the country, from tradition, from the emigration-immigration synonymous with renewed integration into indigenousness. The social efficacy of this heritage can never be overstated. The "Frenchiest" of the French people of colonial origin, the ones that the media present to us as magnificent specimens of "*integration*" are fully penetrated with this history about which they may know nothing. And if they momentarily forget who they are, who they cannot be, the Republic and their white "fellow citizens" are there to remind them. They are not "real" French; their presence in France is illegitimate; the rights they believe they have are not their rights; while they are guilty of no crime, they are guilty of being potentially guilty; they are tolerated; they can even be loved; the hope of "*civilizing*" them is not necessarily lost… but they are Arabs! But they are black! But they are Muslim! An indigenized white person can be de-indigenized; an indigenous person, in the Republic, is irreversibly indigenous. Violence, even when it does not have a taste for the truncheon, is also inherent in post-colonial relationships.

The tendency for young whites in working-class neighborhoods to indigenize does result in the end of racial distinctions, even if they are only reduced in appearance to a mere discrepancy. It generates a complex and fluid combination where common interests and particular or conflicting stakes meet, blend, and are opposed. Often, a same "class condition" carries the social revolt of young inhabitants of the working-class housing projects like the less young; police, cultural, and symbolic violence brings them together without confusing them; they forge reasons for common resistance but they do not eliminate the specific violence to which blacks and Arabs are subjected or that they carry in their memories as descendants of colonized and emigrants-immigrants. And this particular violence determines the demands specific to them, like those related to racial discrimination, to respecting their parents, to repealing double jeopardy or, for Muslims, to having the right to worthy places of prayer or to wear the veil. In reality, even when their demands are identical to those of their white neighbors, well, they are *different*. In advance of their demands, even the most elementary ones, through their resistances, even the most invisible, apolitical in appearance, and sometimes "reactionary" in terms of the binary categories that structure the white political field, their *status* as dominated social race comes into play. They do not formulate it that way, they perhaps do not think it, but the smallest of their protests mobilizes all the accumulated strata of their memory as colonized: the "*hagra*" as the Algerians say. Daughters and sons of emigration-immigration, whether they speak, move, give a reminder of their existence, become visible, raise their head, even more when they get involved in politics, they shake the colonial fetters that call on them to be "polite," stay quiet, be discreet, not show themselves, respect the host's home, accept its traditions, customs and "values," and not get involved in things that do not concern them. And especially no politics, a domain reserved for white citizens, for citizens because they are white, for whites because they are citizens. "*Consider yourselves lucky and shut up!*" is what they are told between two police checks. Not shutting up is "impolite," ungrateful, offensive, "*uncivil*," a characteristic of delinquency, "insecure," an affront to the "national identity," yes, not shutting up is an act of anti-colonial resistance! When they vote for the

Right to punish the PS and PC for their disdain, the indigenous are anti-colonial; when they vote for the Left for fear of the Right, they are anti-colonial; when they no longer believe anything, they remain anti-colonial; when they are "*angry*," when they are "*enraged*," they are still anti-colonial. "*Riots*" are anti-colonial. The massive revolt in November 2005 was definitely anti-colonial. And the Republic knows it!

8

A New Phase in the Colonial Counter-Revolution

> *"But these people are already here," Cleo pointed out. "The ghetto's already formed. The problem now is how best to integrate the people of this ghetto into the life of the community." She turned to me; I'd been silent long enough, "What do you think, Mr. Jones?" "About what?" I asked. She threw a look at me. "I mean what is your opinion as to the problem arising from conditions in Little Tokyo?" Well, sister, you're asking for it, I thought. Aloud I said: "Well, now, I think we ought to kill the colored residents and eat them. In that way we'll not only solve the race problem but alleviate the meat shortage as well." There was a shocked silence [...]"*
> —Chester Himes, *If He Hollers, Let Him Go*, 1945

After the presidential election in May 2007, many questions were asked about the meaning of Sarkozy's overwhelming victory. The head of the

UMP won 53.06% of the vote, one of the best scores for the Right in the Fifth Republic, in a context of very high participation, the highest since the "historic" election of 1981. Sarkozy received support from retired people, farmers, craftspeople, merchants, and executives; he also won more than 40% of the working-class vote (laborers, employees, particularly in suburban residential developments). The defeat of Ségolène Royal was made even worse by the fact that she had benefitted from "tactical voting" on the left, the preceding elections (regional and cantonal) had suggested increased votes for the Socialists, and the final term of Jacques Chirac was characterized by the spread of antiliberal popular protests.[137] In particular, the victory of Nicolas Sarkozy, despite having been Interior Minister in a widely discredited government, broke the cycle of systematic alternation for the first time since the mid-1980s: they vote for the Left and are let down; they vote for the Right and receive blows to the head; they turn back to the Left and it blows up in their face; they vote again for the Right and the cycle continues. In 2007, the working classes took the full brunt of the Right's policies, and yet Sarkozy still won handily. It was a turning point. It cannot be analyzed only in reference to the circumstances of the electoral campaign, the maneuverability of the UMP leader, or the "missteps" of the Socialist candidates.

Attempting to go deeper into things, some commentators discussed in particular the "rightification" of French society, reinforced by the "historic defeat" of the ideas on the left. The "French" would have become more receptive to the "values" of order, security, nation, and economic liberalism incarnated by the new president. Farther to the left, the election results were unsurprising. It was generally a question of the victory of the MEDEF (Movement of Enterprises of France) over the working-classes. More than an evolution of society towards the right, the rallying of the PS to economic liberalism was condemned for preventing the Left from mobilizing its "natural" voters. Basically, the power relations were examined between the working classes and the "power of money" for which Sarkozy was the faithful lapdog and only in that way. All the analyses proposed used a single framework of interpretation: the French political field is split between right and left with, of course, their extremes and their intermediary movements. Yet within this framework itself, there is another common point between all the commentaries provided: Sarkozy won the election because he had the tactical nous to appropriate the main themes of the racist discourse of the Front National. The question that comes first, however, is *why* he was able to do it. Unless we believe that elections are primarily determined by the psychology of the candidates, their opportunism, or their "political courage," we must necessarily ask why, after the "years in the desert" due to his years of support for Balladur against Chirac, was Sarkozy able to establish himself as the main leader on the right, reunify the UMP under his command, and capture a majority of centrists (and Socialists, once he was in power) using a strategy that never hid its intention of recovering racist voters. At the same time, why did Ségolène Royale, without being able to go as far as him in stigmatizing the banlieues and defending the "national identity" nevertheless try to compete with him on this terrain? Why, despite the Right's record and Sarkozy's avowed liberalism, was he able to pull in votes from a large portion of the working classes? Why did nationalists vote massively for a "globalist"? Why did diehard anti-Europeans vote for a fervent pro-European? What is the common denominator between the anti-Americans and Sarkozy's pro-Americanism? The answer is *the defense of white supremacy* on a global level and in hexagonal France. Sarkozy won thanks to a *vote by race*. The right/left divide that had already long been blurred was overshadowed by the social race divide at a level that it had not reached since the Algerian War and triumphant Gaullism. The victory of the Right in 2007 was not the defeat of the Left; it marked a new stage in the construction of the strategic unity of white power that had started with the March for Equality in 1983; it expressed the strong reaction of white working-class resistance to the development of Indigenous Political Power.

Every revolution comes with a counter-revolution. It is almost a historical law. The problem is that we never know where the counter-revolution will come from. Or when. It can emerge from inside the revolution itself. It happens very often. To the point that one is often tempted to renounce the revolution to avoid the counter-revolution. It can appear during, after, and even *before* the revolution. In this latter case, we can speak of a *preventive* counter-revolution (for example, when "independence" was conceded even before anti-colonial protests had become a real threat).

The *first phase of the global anti-colonial revolution*, which reached its peak in the middle of last century, encountered all these forms of counter-revolution. Anti-colonialist forces were able to reconfigure their modes of domination but showed themselves incapable of restoring their full former power. After destroying the American black movement, the United States, which took the relay for the former empires, endeavored to break the liberating momentum of the peoples of Latin America in the first half of the 1970s and fiercely pursued Vietnamese resistance. Israel, for its part, strove to stifle the forces of emancipation of the Arab revolution. These imperialist victories, the effects of which continue to determine global power relations today remain incomplete. The new American empire suffered a sizeable setback in Indochina in 1975. Four years later, the decolonial revolution won a victory in Iran, followed the next year in Nicaragua, and then on the small island of Granada. In new forms, under the impetus of peoples and sometimes states, anti-colonial resistance continued to appear in the countries known as the South, attempting to expand the conquests of the previous period or to preserve its gains in the face of the repeated attempts of White Power to recover what it had lost in terms of political, cultural, and economic control of the people who had gained independence.

From this perspective, the 1980s traced a new global trajectory. The White House, under the direction of Ronald Reagan, first reestablished order in Central America and then helped Saddam Hussein's Iraq in an awful war with Iran. At the same time, it deployed elements of the economic war called "globalization" of which the IMF,[138] the World Bank, and many other regional agreements were—and still are—the instruments. However, these were only the preliminaries of the *second phase of the colonial counter-revolution* that took on its full scope with the implosion of the Soviet empire in 1989. Two years later, there was the first Iraq War. The decisive commitment came after September 11, 2001 with the intervention in Afghanistan, the occupation of Iraq, the deadly offensives by the Israeli army in Palestine and Lebanon, and the threats of military intervention against Iran. The epicenter of the colonial counter-revolution is in the Middle East, where it is most clearly and most violently expressed, but it is also active in other forms (economic, military, political, "psychological"…) on every continent, as much in the southern hemisphere of the Americas (Venezuela, Bolivia) as in Asia and Africa, especially in the Sahel. Under the leadership of the United States, with unconditional support from Israel and Great Britain and support from the main European states as well as the more or less enthusiastic participation of other countries, this second phase of the colonial counter-revolution is preventive to the extent that it seeks to stifle the processes of decolonial resistance that were rekindled over the last decade of the last century. It also represents a reaction against the accumulation of power by certain formerly dominated states (China, in particular). And especially, an old objective now seems possible since the fall of the USSR: without calling into question the state mechanisms established on the ruins of colonial administrations, except temporarily (as in Iraq), the aim is to eliminate the leverage that allowed some of them to gain a margin of sovereignty in relation to white powers. The second phase of the colonial counter-revolution is therefore offensive as well. It is the recolonization of the world in a world that has not stopped being colonial. But it is not only that. Like the previous colonial enterprises, it is also *antagonism within White Power over sharing the world*. An unbalanced dispute in the context of power relations that still largely favors North America, a muted confrontation that prefers economic and political instruments, that only expresses itself through violence indirectly, in the form of instrumentalizing rivalries and wars inside the dominated countries, the current colonial counter-revolution is also a conflict internal to the white world. Through these antagonisms, in the same way as during the first colonial expansion following the "discovery" of the American continent or the establishment of the major empires starting in the nineteenth century, the entire global system of states is reconfigured along with sovereignties, nations, spheres of influence and authority, and identities.

The colonial counter-revolution is also expressed in the internal struggles and social confrontations that affect each state; it develops at the intersection of multiple planetary issues. We should, however, avoid muddying the dirty waters of the "complexity" that is systematically thrown back at us to prevent us from being able to tell our friends (even our temporary friends) from our foes. Beyond their disputes, the consolidation of white strategic unity represents the "priority of priorities" for "civilized" states. The colonial counter-revolution underway is a war to preserve or reinforce the *statutory* (political, cultural, moral, economic…) domination of one part of the world, a planetary white-European-Christian aristocracy, the "white supermen," as Gramsci put it, over all others. Its first codename is "war of civilizations," the modern and democratic West against the archaic and despotic Orient, the enlightened Christian world against the obscurantist Muslim world, aimed at rekindling the white supremacist consciousness. Its second pseudonym is the "war on terror" aimed at reigniting feelings of insecurity among the white *minority* against the barbarian indigenous *majority*.

Sarkozy was the first head of state since de Gaulle to be elected so that France could play its role in the colonial counter-revolution. There is no other way to explain how Sarkozy, continuing the endeavors of Jacques Chirac, was successful in uniting the Right under his leadership and leading it to victory, how he was able to sow discord on the left, in particular among the PS, from which he was able to steal some leaders for his first government than the hegemony of powers in France for which the defense of the white world was a central objective. Sarkozy made it one of his key themes. Despite some nuances over the role of France in the global White Power, the main French political forces agree on this goal that specifically involves consolidating relations with the United States and more direct support of the war waged by the colonial state of Israel on the Palestinian people (whether this war takes the form of a direct military engagement or a "peace process"). *It is the eighth axis around which white consensus is built.* Nevertheless, this strategic consensus did not develop solely in function of the parameters of the international situation. It was supported—and maintained—by white working-class resistance inside the borders of hexagonal France itself. The ideology of the "clash of civilizations" resonates so much in France because, as we have seen, the white masses in the country are confronted with the progress of Indigenous Power in their immediate environment. Along with the rise of the indigenous "at home," the deterioration of their social conditions, unemployment, the breakdown of citizenship, the erosion of cultural markers, the degradation of their symbolic status as French or whites appear to them more or less confusedly as the result of indigenous pressure on a global scale. "Insecurity" on the RER D train line seems to them to be the corollary of the "insecurity" that the indigenous supposedly impose on the world. The Arabs, Blacks, and Muslims that drain white privilege in France become, in their eyes, the expression of an indigenous peril on a global scale, an "internal enemy" in the proper sense of the term. In a certain way, they express an awareness that hexagonal white privilege *is* planetary white privilege; that social gains, security, and democracy in countries of the North are to a large extent the product of poverty, insecurity, despotism, maintained by White Power in countries in the South. Here again, the "false consciousness" is also a "real" consciousness. Because, as Frantz Fanon stressed, "Europe's well-being and progress were built with the sweat and corpses of blacks, Arabs, Indians, and Asians."[139] He added, "This we are determined never to forget." We have not forgotten it. But it so happens that Europeans have not forgotten it either, even though they feign not to know anything about it.

This racial consciousness, sustained by the "government parties"—I should say "state parties" to the extent that they are, in reality, part of the state—encounters the intrinsic interests of the French state, faced with the new threats that weigh on the stability of the republican pact on which it is based. Its first serious crisis, provoked by the German occupation and the establishment of the

Vichy regime, was resolved after the war by the national-colonial union around de Gaulle. The second shock, decolonization, by necessity, once again under the patronage of the general—the only one capable of reestablishing national union—was a profound reworking of the parameters of the republican pact. The third shock was the discovery, starting in the 1980s, that France was now black, Arab, and Muslim. The massive presence of blacks and Arabs and their sudden intrusion into the political field blew up the contradictions of a nationality seen as both "citizen" and "Gallic," white and Christian. Definitively established in France, socialized in France, and often French, the children of immigrants have exposed the racial mechanisms of citizenship.

This internal indigenous power might also have seemed formidable because it appeared in a context affected by other changes that had disturbed the national-racist cohesion. France's involvement in competition in the white world, in the context of the colonial counter-revolution, opens other fault lines in the republican pact. The first of these consequences, following the growing ascendancy of the United States stimulated by the colonial counter-revolution, is the ongoing erosion of France's political position in the world, in other words the deterioration of the imperial ambitions on which its "national identity" was largely based.

The second consequence is the rapid—albeit still relative—empowerment in relation to the state of the largest French companies, now multinationals or involved in the logics of the globalized market. The state's control of the economic leverage that constitutes one of the instruments of its force and its independence, in other words its sovereignty, was considerably weakened. Fashioned in the context of the imperial expansion of the nation, the nation-state enters into crisis in the context of the neoliberal dissolution of the nation.

Instrument of war aimed at subjugating and pillaging the states of the South, liberal globalization is also a weapon to break working-class resistance in the heart of the imperial metropolises and call into question the social gains won/conceded over the decades that followed World War II. It breaks apart the social dimension of the republican pact, and is intimately associated, as we have seen, with its national and racial dimensions: French and white privilege is constitutive of social privilege. What knits together the "French nation" and serves as the basis for real citizenship, from which indigenous people are excluded, is the articulation built and guaranteed by the Republic between the fact of being able to access some social benefits and the qualities of French people and whites. For this reason, the gradual dismantling of social advantages also shakes up the national matrix in which they participate. Reshaping the constitutive dimensions of the republican pact then appears to become an imperative for the state. It is one of the major foundations for the combination between consensus on questions of immigration built since the 1980s between the main white forces, and consensus on economic liberalism. From this point of view, socioeconomic questions do not exist outside the national-racial question. The central political issue today is not only more or less economic liberalism but the future of the Republic itself.

As equally crucial an issue as the ongoing movement of racialization was precipitated by the construction of Europe, which has also contributed to the disintegration of the republican pact in its social, citizen, and national dimensions, while suggesting the possibility of a partial alternative in white "Europeanness." Cause and result of liberal globalization and the reclassification within international White Power, the acceleration of European construction is accompanied by an accentuation of racial differentiation, as much within the limits of the European Union as within the borders of the Hexagon. European construction altered the national element of the republican pact, but its primary effects are complex, both antagonistic and complementary: on one hand, it fans the French nationalism of part of the population (leading to the "no" of the far right on the European Constitution), a nationalism of which the enclosure as European, white, and Christian is a part; on the other, it tends to strengthen, within another part of the population (that voted "yes" on the European Constitution), this identity bound around the enclosure as European, white, and Christian that breaks the shell of French nationalism. An equation that is all the more difficult to resolve in that the European Union is only a liberal technocratic machine; "European citizenship," already very restricted, is without social mediations. It is therefore indispensable for asserting itself, if not for constituting a European state, to be articulated around a form of transnational identity of which the main point of support is the identification between Europeanness, whiteness, and Christianity, all of which are assimilated with the Greco-Latin "birthplace" of "Western civilization," "modernity" and the reign of freedoms, human rights and… anti-racism or, more precisely, the anti-"Muslim antisemitism!"[140] The European Union prolongs the historical process of white affirmation described by Étienne Balibar: "The colonial castes of the various nationalities (British, French, Dutch, Portuguese, and so on) *worked together* to forge the idea of 'White' superiority, of civilization as an interest that has to be defended against the savages. This representation—'the White man's burden'—has contributed in a decisive way to molding the modern notion of a supranational European or Western identity."[141] The transnational, racial, and "European identity" is therefore constructed in the global colonial counter-revolution. It is closed, like a statuary ensemble, through an architecture that associates the construction of fortifications on its borders—fortifications in which the Maghreb states participate by rejecting, assaulting, and sometimes even killing sub-Saharan migrants—with the establishment of what Balibar calls a "European apartheid" that takes form in the multiplication of structures of exclusion, repression, and insecurity of black, Arab, and Muslim migrations as in the consecration of the statutory privilege represented by the "European citizenship" from which the new European indigenous (*indigénat*) is excluded. And it is precisely through its integration in the European process that the French state seeks to rebuild the constitutive dimensions of the republican pact. René Gallissot had already suggested after the March for Equality that "The current slide into 'cultural' racism—even the human rights that become indicators of Western superiority—suggests that national identity began to lose its virtue following the transnationalization that is spreading with decolonization and migrations; it becomes useful to double it with an identity of a 'cultural nature':

the defense of French identity and European identity at the same time, and the superiority of civilization that its essence confers on it by heritage."[142]

At the intersection of several, sometimes contradictory issues, the colonial counter-offensive in France aims to reorganize the republican pact and plug its holes. Its social dimensions have not yet lost all their functionality (working-class resistance in fact hampers their dismantling); the institution known as "nation" is not yet obsolete; the mechanisms of citizenship continue to play a partial role as integrators; however, the elements of crisis are already there, the various mechanisms of the republican pact are rusty and their gears are jammed. One of the fundamental dimensions of the state's strategy to fix it consists of readjusting the components of the republican pact by asserting a dimension that is both at the heart of French nationalism and goes far beyond it, that is in accordance with European construction and with liberal-colonial globalization: white supremacy. It does not mean—and we should insist on this point—that Franco-Gallic nationalism has been consigned to history. I nevertheless think that the connection between these two, partially antagonistic dimensions that constitute the French "national identity," Franco-centrism, and White-centrism tend to change in favor of the latter.

It is the hegemonic strategy currently at the heart of white power. It is, of course, the choice of Nicolas Sarkozy and the majority on the right. It is also the predominant trend within the PS apparatus, buttressed by its tens of thousands of municipal officials and its representatives in the multitude of machines of state power. Competing with the Right for control of the state and with other lefts for control of the Left, torn by internal antagonism, subject to the refractory pressure of white working-class resistance within it, forced to take into account a fraction of its voting base that is concerned by the dismantling of the social dimension of the republican pact, forced to preserve at least a semblance of the "socialist humanism" that constitutes its partisan identity, the PS has more difficulties than the Right in explicitly defining a political orientation and implementing it when in power. More than the Right, its strategies are fleeting, sinuous, full of contradictions, formulated in euphemistic and careful ways, and put into practice in a gradual, muted, and indirect manner. Some choices, however, now hegemonic at the center of the Socialist apparatus, have been clearly asserted over the years, highlighting the fundamental affinities within White Power that go beyond its divisions.

The election of Sarkozy therefore represented a new stage in the racial offensive against the indigenous.

Nevertheless, the crossed currents of power relations, their instability, the existence of forces that oppose the rebuilding of the republican pact around a racial axis in the white political field, and the persistent wavering of the working-class consciousness can still slow or even reverse this process. The decolonization of French society, however, will not occur if the indigenous fail to establish themselves as an autonomous political power.

Heading into the Waves...

"What he doesn't say, the fedayee [...] is that he knows that he himself will not see this revolution accomplished, but that his own victory is to have begun it."

—Jean Genet

"And you'll always be a slave as long as you're trying to be responsible and respectable in the eyesight of your master; you'll remain a slave. When you're in the eyesight of your master, you've got to let him know you're irresponsible and you'll blow his irresponsible head off."

—Malcolm X, 1965

Anger is rising among us. An anger too often dulled by resentment. Because pessimism is rampant. Defeatism. Disarray. I cannot say that these feelings are unjustified. But I cannot say that they are justified either. The colonial counter-revolution is asserting itself. However, Indigenous Political Power is not growing weaker. It is not a question of being blind to our own weaknesses but of knowing what they are and recognizing how far we have come in less than thirty years. After all, we started with almost nothing! In a way, the whites are not wrong to say that we are too impatient. The older generations, or "*chibani*," did not know that many of them would end their lives in France. They worked hard, they had to be strong against humiliations to survive. They did not know that their children would become French or that they would be French without being French. Their struggles in the 1970s, as determined as they were, were only a preliminary, only a vague outline of what independent Indigenous Power would be. The new indigenous generations born in France, excluded from the political system like their immigrant elders, had to invent everything. First, they had to know themselves before knowing their enemy. They had to discover themselves as power before building their power. They had to understand their political specificity before entering politics, reflect on the thinking of others before thinking for themselves, test the political tools available to them before moving beyond them. And the same is true today to an extent. Despite its illusions in the Republic, the ambivalence, and deception that followed, the March for Equality and Against Racism was the true birth of indigenous politics. And White Power did not fail to recognize it. But we did, and far too often! Behind the defeats, the "appropriations," the decomposition of the most resolute indigenous movements, the general dispersion, the short-lived protests, and the quickly suppressed riots, we have not always seen the groundswell that had already begun. We have not always seen the advances coming in the midst of retreats; we have confused political and organizational experiments, explorations, incursions into the unknown, taking risks, improvisation, and shifting front lines with disorder, "immaturity," divisions, confusion, risky ventures, and other reasons for despair. Our necessary arguments have appeared to us like children's squabbling or the expression of plots fomented by an omniscient foe capable of controlling, absorbing, and destroying everything. We have not always recognized the atypical, contradictory, non-"French" forms through which our resistance was built. We have been lost in the winding paths that the indigenous consciousness took before crystallizing into political power. Caught in the whirlpool of our contradictory dynamics, we have turned to landmarks that were not our own to guide us. In short, we have all too often looked at politics, *our* politics, through white eyes. Our eyes are indigenous; they suffered colonization, they learned to see in French schools, so be it! But then let's praise strabismus, let's look this way, cross-eyed, out of sync, discordant. Let's look past the Whites.

We will see, of course, that White Power still has immeasurably more force than our power. That this force penetrates us through and through. That we are surrounded inside and out. That it multiplies its violence and malignancy as soon we lift our heads. However, we will also see that White Power is torn by its own antagonisms. That it is always victorious but has suffered terrible defeats. That it reigns over us less by its brutality than by our illusions. Fundamentally, it is completely rotten, but we don't recognize it. Too many of us dream of resembling it, but how could they admit that they want to resemble rot? White men went to the moon, let's go to the moon, they think. But how many human disasters had to occur for men to go to the moon? How many human disasters did this "great step for mankind" announce? Going to the moon is rotten. Our liberation will not consist of imitating the whites.

This is not what I wanted to discuss here. Instead, it is weakness that we have to detect at the heart of White Power. And that we will not see as long as we remain fascinated by its power. In the same way that we do not see our own power as long as it does not tell us: "It is true, finally you exist, you represent something, you have a certain force." It is what Sarkozy did by naming three indigenous ministers. And many of us were satisfied: "If there is an Arab minister, it means that I, an Arab, exist!" "If there is a black minister, it means that I, a black person, exist!" Moreover, in a certain way, it is true: White Power named indigenous ministers because it is aware that our force as a nuisance is not negligible; during the last elections, we saw "candidates of diversity" blossom on white lists because they now have to deal with us. Would we have seen so many white parties come for our votes if there had not been the 2005 revolt? Would Sarkozy have called on Dati-Amara-Yade if, more clairvoyant no doubt than others, he had not understood that we could not be avoided? Jean Genet: "we have perfected an imposture in the grand style: to a few carefully chosen blacks we have granted celebrity status, and we have multiplied their image, but only so that they will remain what we ask them to be: actors and comedians."[143] Of course there is "appropriation," of course involving some of ours in their positions of power, giving them a role in the republican theater hides the reality of racial policies, sows illusions; clearly, promoting a well-integrated, indigenous elite means creating an intermediate category, half-oppressed, half-privileged, impatient to make others forget where they came from by walking over our bodies if necessary. "The Colored, of South Africa, for example, are—or were—a legal creation: *half-breeds*, or *mulattoes*, to use the elegant and civilized terms of the Civilized—people pale enough to hope to be treated as White. Or, surrendering the hope of an earthly paradise, at least not to be treated as Black. This aspiration, during their purgatory—so it was hoped and intended—would cause them to ally themselves with White Power instead of Black insurrection."[144] But the "emancipated" (Toussaint Louverture was one...[145]), the "mulattoes," the "mixed-race," the partially citizenized indigenous, the "*beur*"-ified Arabs, and the "Roselmacked" Blacks have always been two-edged swords. Both for the oppressors *and* for the oppressed. White Power knows it and only grants certain privileges to some of us drop by drop and only when it fears the majority of us. The increase in the number of "handy *beurs*" is just as much the result of their—sometimes cynical—efforts to get by as it is the authorities' awareness of our growing power. We, however, only see the blows we receive. Not always? Too often. We see the hatred we elicit, Islamophobia, Negrophobia; we see police numbers increase, repression spread, mechanisms of control and surveillance strengthened, structures of corruption and cronyism flourish, and bodies of institutionalization, integration, and supervision develop, but we do not see the cause, or one of the causes, which is none other than the threat that we now pose to the white order. "If someone has bitten you," goes the proverb, "he has reminded you that you have teeth," and our teeth are much sharper than we think. When white forces try to appropriate our votes during elections, when they engage with the question of racism, when they redirect our resistance in function of their own issues, when they absorb some of our militants, we generally only see them as maneuvers and attempts to break up our independent struggles. We do not see it as a testament to the progress in our power. We see that immigration, banlieues, and national identity occupy an increasingly larger place in the conflicts within White Power, that Sarkozy was elected *against* us, that Ségolène Royale would have like to have been elected for the same reason, but, paradoxically, instead of seeing it as the result of our mobilization or even simply as the *political* reflection of our increasingly active presence, our increasingly significant presence in every realm of social life, we are tempted to see it as the expression of our vulnerability. Of course, during the last presidential election, the colonialist pole intensified its efforts; it was brutally evident in the campaigns of the main parties; as for us, we were once again absent as an independent political power; the relationship of forces seemed to oppose white forces against each other. Even diluted, indigenous resistance nevertheless expressed itself through the white parties. Most of those among us who voted for the PS did not do it because they hoped for an improvement in their lives but to stand in the way of the most extreme tendencies of the colonialist pole. Others voted for Sarkozy; not because they were enthusiastic about the idea of defending the "national identity" with him, but on the contrary because they thought they saw him as a candidate who would respect their Muslim identity. Many others voted for Bayrou, not because they were seduced by his centrist bleating, but under the illusion that he could break up the left-right alternation that they knew was only an alternation between factions of White Power. However, independently of the rigged electoral choices through which indigenous resistance had to express itself, if the "indigenous question" represented a major issue in the election campaign, if it determined the results of the vote, it can only be for the following two reasons: 1) the force of white resistance is growing; 2) the force of indigenous resistance is growing.

It should be noted that I am not claiming we have a political power that is conscious of itself and capable of acting independently. We are not there yet. Our political power is often manifested in relief, by its effects more than its "display"; it is diffuse, discontinuous, and chaotic. I would say that, despite our weakness, we already represent a force capable of determining issues in the political field and that this force, far from diminishing over the years, has continued to assert itself in forms and with content that we do not always master, through mediations that often surprise us, sometimes in independent spaces, sometimes not, or attempting to take on White Power indirectly. We do not see its scope every time. Some of us are mistaken when they confuse our political power with its autonomous and radical expression alone. But this expression is in fact quite meager. It is and will remain for a long time in the minority. The great majority of us are and will remain for a time and to different degrees in the grasp of integrationist illusions characteristic of the status of the colonized. For now, Indigenous Power, far from being built independently, is being built in the dominant political and ideological frameworks, much more often in heteronomy than autonomy. Even more, it is being built to a large extent through the institutions of the adversary. And yet, should it be understood in its entirety, with appreciation of its paradoxes, the unequal rhythms of development of the different sectors where it is constituted, its different terrains of action, the different modalities through which it is embodied, Indigenous Power is there, it asserts itself, it proliferates, it *disturbs*. It disturbs to the extent that it *exists* and to the extent that it *could exist*. Our growing *social* power is already a *political* power. Our *democratic* reality is *already* a *political* reality. We have passed the "tolerance threshold!" We are increasingly present, present everywhere, and not only in the most odious factories and neighborhoods; we are leading struggles; we are changing France; our real and potential political power therefore *deserves* to be destroyed. In this sense, the colonial counter-revolution is also preventive.

We persist in thinking that the retreat of some "traditional" forms of mobilization, the breakdown of some spaces of resistance that were at the front line of combats, the disengagement of many militants, the "neighborhoodist" contraction, and dispersion necessarily imply a degradation of the relationship of forces. It is the case and it is not the case. I have tried to show it in this book. Or at least to suggest that the March in December 1983 opened a new period marking the upward rise of Indigenous Political Power; a muddled, non-linear and non-homogenous growth, entering unexpected spaces, according to forms that have been called "infra-political" but for which the causes and effects are fully political, a growth that is clearly far from being autonomous, but already capable of acting on the relationships of forces. The racial political divide has become central without erasing the other divides, determining the strategies of the different actors, upsetting equilibriums, provoking reconstructions of the political field, convergences, and new conflicts, that would not be intelligible without accounting for the resurgence of indigenous resistance. An exhaustive analysis of all the forms of struggle and sedition, their real dynamics, their ambivalences, the profound meaning of each shift of the front lines remains to be done. I have only sketched out a potential path in the previous pages. The rough outline that I feel I have been able to trace is insufficient. The white counter-offensive also requires much more astute study than I am able to perform now. What seems most important to me, however, is to attempt to break the ideological matrix in which the Republic ensnares our creative imagination, in other words our politics.

Because if there is a reason that prevents us from appreciating the reality of power relations, it is, in the first place, that we do not see them as power relations between White Power and Indigenous Political Power but as a multiplicity of disconnected power relations that evolve along parallel lines or at least, that only intersect rarely, expressing the fundamentally heterogeneous interests of "social categories" or disparate communities, or even of portions of the population with one "mentality" or another, one "ideology" or another. There would therefore be power relations opposing racists and anti-racists, power relations opposing Islamophobes and Muslims, power relations opposing "descendants of immigration" and *souchiens*, Domiens, and Hexagonals, neighborhoods and non-neighborhoods, "appropriated" and fierce defenders of autonomy, and more; all these power relations finally participating in a political matrix structured by the power relations between right and left. There is clearly some truth here. The dominant reading grids of the conflicts that mask the colonial-racial are imposed on us as the very effect of this facture in social and institutional reality. The separation of the different indigenous communities is not an illusion; it is the product of their different historical paths, overdetermined—and sometimes produced—by colonial reality and aggravated by the conditions of their integration in France. Similarly, the state territorializes social racial inequalities by relegating the banlieues and, at the same time, it territorializes the space of resistance. The Republic, established on the foundation of frontiers and nationality, distinguishes foreigners from nationals, determining divergent interests. It is also true that economic differentiation, and the opposition between right and left that refracts it in part, is a strong determinant of the structure of the political field.

However, the reflection in our heads of this part of truth is also an internalization of the gaze that white common sense, constructed by the colonial Republic, casts on the social reality of our struggles.

They tell us that colonial domination was only a parenthesis, and now part of history. You do not exist as dominated races whose actions produce power relations, but as an abundance of minorities and "social categories," each with its own very unique expectations. While this statement comes from the most perfect hypocrisy on the part of the state and government political forces, for the white, anti-racist forces, republican blindness arrives at the same conclusion: there is no conflict of races but of the specific, more or less legitimate causes of different communities or different social groups with no relationship between each other. The nicest of them, at least those who do not reduce everything to socioeconomic issues, offer us a stupid "convergence of minorities," as if the political divide opposed a "normed" majority with minorities "outside the norm." Wanting to make our struggles merely a dimension of one of the other divides that split society is one of the weapons used—naively or cynically, it doesn't matter—by white forces to prohibit us from seeing the unity of the colonized condition and the fundamental convergence of our dynamics of resistance. It prohibits us from thinking Indigenous Power.

Each indigenous group, convinced it is leading the struggle on its own, only for its objectives, becomes blind to the racial reality of the whole of which it is a part; it can only evaluate the power relations and its own power from its unique situation, a small national, cultural, or "territorial" minority lost in a million other minorities, each apparently just as powerless. And, just to use one example, few "rascals" from indigenous neighborhoods see the connections between their anger against the police and the struggles of undocumented immigrant workers, or the struggles of workers against racial discrimination, or even the struggles of the descendants of African deportees calling for reparations.

By understanding our struggles from a postcolonial and racial perspective, another reality is revealed: the profound unity between the social and political logic of these struggles, the fact that the entire movement of these resistances follows a same logic of opposing white domination and forms a totality, Indigenous Political Power.

"*Heading into the waves, negotiating them* exact, *using their opposing unleashed energies to head up and across.*"[146]

Notes

Introduction: Apocalyptic Times

1. James Baldwin, *The Evidence of Things Not Seen* (New York: Holt, Rinehart, and Winston, 1985), 18.

2. It is the title of a luminous article by Abdelmalek Sayad, recently republished in the book *Immigration ou les paradoxes de l'alterité; . 2. Les enfants illégitimes* (Paris: Raisons d'agir, 2006), 13–44. Written in 1985, this text was inspired by the December 1983 March for Equality and Against Racism.

3. Translator's note: To quote Selim Nadi: "the word '*indigène*' is not easy to translate into English without emptying it of its political substance. But even if 'indigenous' is not the best translation for the French word '*indigène*,' I will use it here for reasons of simplicity […]. But keep in mind that the French word is referring to the concept of the colonial subject." Preliminary comments to his talk "Why do we need an Indigenous Party in France?" presented at the Eleventh Annual Historical Materialism Conference at SOAS University of London (http://indigenes-republique.fr/why-do-we-need-an-indigenous-party-in-france/).

4. Translator's note: The word "banlieue" in French refers to the suburbs of a large city, but since the 1970s, it has also referred more specifically, in France, to working-class suburban areas with low-income housing projects (HLM).

5. Hugh Thomas, *The Slave Trade: The Story of the Atlantic Slave Trade: 1440–1870* (New York: Simon & Schuster, 1997), 541.

6. William Lloyd Garrison, "An address, delivered before the free people of color, in Philadelphia, New-York, and other cities, during the month of June, 1831" (Boston: Stephen Foster, 1831) [http://www.loc.gov/resource/rbaapc.10700], cited in Françoise

Vergès, *Abolir l'esclavage: une utopie colonial. L'ambiguïté d'une politique humanitaire. Textes et entretiens* (Paris: Gallimard, 1991).

7. Jean Genet, "For George Jackson," *The Declared Enemy: Texts and Interviews* (Stanford, CA: Stanford University Press, 2004), 68.

8. Jean Genet, "*Introduction* to Soledad Brother," *The Declared Enemy*, 54.

9. Kwame Ture [Stokely Carmichael] and Charles V. Hamilton, "II, Black Power: It's Need and Substance," *Black Power: The Politics of Liberation in America. With New Afterwords by the Authors* (New York, NY: Vintage Books, 1992), 35. I will never tire of quoting black American authors. They are not only speaking about America, they are speaking about us. Maybe about all colonized peoples. They might not know it but when we read them, we the indigenous in France are immediately overwhelmed by deep feelings of gratitude and recognition. In all meanings of the words: they are writing our lives, our experiences, our struggles, and our dreams. Some sociologist or another might say it is mere illusion. But those sociologists are idiots. Before opening their mouth, and getting all excited at their keyboard, they should have asked themselves if this kind of "elective affinity" is only the product of chance or of our twisted brains. Incidentally, there are probably enlightened bleeding hearts on the other side of the Atlantic who would begrudge black activists for quoting *The Wretched of the Earth*: "Fanon is speaking of colonial Algeria, what does that have to do with us?"

10. Of course, this book does not speak for the Movement of the Indigenous of the Republic, even though I am a member of that group. However, it owes much to the Movement. The experience I gained there, the many activists that it has given me the opportunity to meet—and whom I'd like to thank here for everything they have given me—the discussions and reflections in which I participated have indeed been indispensable to my own thinking. The following pages extend the development I began in an essay called "Towards a Politics of the Rabble. Immigrants, Indigenous and Youth from the banlieue," published as *Pour une politique de la racaille. Immigré-e-s, Indigènes et jeunes de banlieue.* (Paris: Editions Textuel, 2006). I will not revisit here a number of questions that

were already discussed in that book except in passing to introduce additional nuances or minor corrections.

11. Edouard Glissant, "Supposez le vol de milliers d'oiseaux sur un lac africain" in *Outre-mers, notre monde. Entretiens d'Oudinot* (Paris: Autrement, 2002), 15.

1. The Proof of Social Races Is in Their Struggle!

12. Karl Marx and Frederick Engels, *The German Ideology. Part One, With Selections from Parts Two and Three and Supplementary Texts Together with Marx's "Introduction to a Critique of Political Economy,"* Ed. C.J. Arthur (New York: International Publishers, 2004), 45.

13. Around 1440, "the seizure of slaves, rather than their purchase, was then a frequent practice in both Europe and Africa. These 'razzias,' as the odious practice of man-stealing was known, were carried out throughout the Middle Ages in Spain and Africa by Muslim merchants, and their Christian equivalents had done the same. Muslims were justified by the Koran in seizing Christians and enslaving them; the Christians, in their long-drawn-out reconquest of Muslim Spain, had conducted themselves similarly." Hugh Thomas, *The Slave Trade: The Story of the Atlantic Slave Trade: 1440–1870* (New York: Simon & Schuster, 1997), 23.

14. James Baldwin, *The Evidence of Things not Seen*, 30.

15. Idem.

16. It seems legitimate to wonder if there isn't a link between this conception of the world and Marx's recurrent assertions from *The German Ideology* to the *Grundisse* stating that the passage from barbarism to civilization occurs in the separation of the city and the country.

17. Hugh Thomas, in *The Slave Trade*, also finds a plausible explanation for this phenomenon in the drying up of the other sources of procurement following the end of the wars of conquest on the borders of Europe.

18. "Slavery is inscribed in the law: by the Act to Regulate the Negroes on the Plantations (1667) in the British colonies, by the Code Noir (1685) in the French colonies, and by the Codigos

Negros (1768) in the Spanish colonies." (Françoise Vergès, *Abolir l'esclavage*, 45.)

19. Ibid., 44.

20. Ibid., 45.

21. Danielle Lochak, "La *race*: une catégorie juridique?," in *Mots*, "Races," (1992) vol. 3, 1.

22. Ibid.

23. "In all the colonies with slavery, relations between whites and blacks quickly became the object of fastidious attention and soon prohibited by law, from the earliest period of colonization. The typology of mixing and the abundance of names to which it gave rise reveal the complexity of the phenomenon. How can the portion of white blood that an individual could claim be evacuated? What should it be called? Several terms were invented at the time: *Sacatra* [one black and one griffe parent], *griffe* [three-quarter black and one-quarter white], *marabou* [offspring of mulatto and griffe], *sang-mêlé* [mixed blood], *octavon* [octoroon, mustee], *quarteron* [quadroon], *mulâtre* [mulatto], *zambo* [sambo]. This toponymy claims to define not only the genotype and phenotype of a person, but also their psychological specificities, in particular the flaws associated with each type." Françoise Vergès, *Abolir l'esclavage*, 50.

24. Domenico Losurdo, *Le péché originel du XXe siècle* (Brussels: éditions Aden, 2007 (1998)), 19 and 21.

25. George M. Frederickson, *Racism: A Short History* (Princeton and Oxford: Princeton University Press, 2002), 47.

26. George M. Frederickson, *Racism: A Short History*, 104–5.

27. I am speaking here about democratization and not pseudo-democratization. Democracy, like the republic, is nothing other than its real form of existence. I am emphasizing this point because I often hear it said that democracy in France is not a "real" democracy, that the Socialist Party is not socialist, that the Communist Party is not communist, or that the Left is not really on the left. Let's suppose that Plato, Rousseau, Robespierre or Marx had written, "Sheep are ovines who have the distinctive characteristic of having five feet."

Upon returning from an agricultural show, one of their adepts would no doubt say, "How strange, there were no sheep. I only saw so-called sheep, supposed sheep, sheep in quotes, or traitors to sheepness." It is the same as when we say that the republic is not the republic, or when the Left is not the Left.

28. See Emmanuelle Saada, *Empire's Children: Race, Filiation, and Citizenship in the French Colonies* (Chicago, Ill: University of Chicago Press, 2012) and Carole Reynaud Paligot, *La république raciale: paradigme racial et idéologie républicaine (1860–1930)* (Paris: Presses Universitaires de France, 2009).

29. Abdelmalek Sayad. "Les enfants illégitimes" (1979) in *L'immigration ou les paradoxes de l'altérité*, 166.

30. Angela Davis, *Abolition Democracy: Beyond Empire, Prisons, and Torture* (New York: Seven Stories Press, 2005), 57.

31. Kwame Ture [Stokely Carmichael] and Charles V. Hamilton, *Black Power: The Politics of Liberation in America. With New Afterwords by the Authors* (New York: Vintage, 1992), 3–4.

2. The Republic Is a Liar

32. Gérard Noiriel, *Immigration, antisémitisme et racisme en France: XIXe-XXe siècle: discours publics, humiliations privées* (Paris: Fayard, 2007), 192.

33. We can see that, on the level of discourse, it is false to assert that the specifically French conception of the nation is almost the complete opposite of the German one. This latter, "ethnic," conception considers the nation to be an immemorial, objective reality founded on a natural community whose members descend from the same ancestors (*jus sanguinis*, or citizenship by blood) and whose spirit or nature is expressed in its culture and its language. In fact, each of these conceptions were constructed through the other and in opposition to one another and tend to merge.

34. Things were not that simple, however. The Third Republic was the theater of conflicts of interest, political conflicts, and social and ideological confrontations, quite often violent, around these policies. It can be seen, for example, with the Dreyfus Affair, which saw the defeat of the more antisemitic strains. Yet the fact remains

that it was concretely instituted and constitutes the historical track record of the Third Republic.

35. Étienne Balibar, M. Chemillier-Gendreau, J. Costa-Lascoux, and E. Terray, *Sans-papiers: l'archaïsme fatal*, Paris: La Découverte, 1999, 76.

36. Aimé Césaire and Françoise Vergès, *Nègre je suis, nègre je resterai: entretiens avec Françoise Vergès* (Paris: Albin Michel, 2005).

37. Étienne Balibar and Immanuel Maurice Wallerstein, *Race, nation, classe: les identités ambiguës* (Paris: Editions La Découverte, 1998).

3. Why We Should Hate Charles de Gaulle

38. Translator's note: Algeria was long considered a French province and partitioned into three "departments" with the same administrative structure as the departments of metropolitan France.

39. Michel Winock, *L'agonie de la IVe République: 13 mai 1958.* (Paris: Gallimard, 2013), 277.

40. Ibid, 281.

41. "At the heart of the community, the constitution provides that common responsibilities (broadly viewed) will be carried out by different bodies—the community senate, the executive council, the arbitration tribunal, the president of the Community—all dominated by the French state. Two-thirds of the senate was composed of French delegates, the president of the Community was the president of the French Republic, the arbitration tribunal is appointed by the president, and the executive council can only discuss the president's decisions, a president elected by an association of dignitaries of which overseas members can comprise no more than 5%." Hugues Portelli, *La Ve République* (Paris: Grasset, 1994), 69.

42. Jean Nanga notes that, "despite the many revisions (eight, to be exact) of the constitution of the Fifth Republic, the French legislation only repealed the community in 1995!" Jean Nanga, "FrançAfrique; les ruses de la raison postcoloniale" [French Africa: the Ruses of Post-colonial Reason] in "Postcolonialisme et Immigration," ed. Sadri Khiari and Nicolas Qualander, special issue, *ContreTemps*, no. 16 (January 2006): 114.

43. Translator's note: The Rally of the French People (Rassemblement du Peuple Français, RPF) was the political party founded by De Gaulle in 1947 that advocated for revising the constitutional in view of a presidential government.

44. Here are some examples from the Gaullist period. In Cameroon, the separatist leader Ruben Um Nyobé was killed by French troops on September 13, 1958. His successor, Félix Moumié, would be assassinated during France's participation in the extremely deadly war waged by the regime it had put in place against the Union of the Peoples of Cameroon (Union des Populations du Cameroun, UPC). Togo achieved independence on April 27, 1960 after a referendum won by the Committee of Togolese Unity (Comité de l'unité togolaise, CUT) led by Sylvanus Olympio, who became president of the republic. He was not particularly radical. And yet France instigated his assassination in January 1963. France would replace him with a puppet ruler, who would be followed by the infamous dictator Étienne Eyadéma. The Côte d'Ivoire gained independence in 1960, and France placed its protégé Houphouët Boigny at its head. It would of course assist him in cleaning out all of those who'd been involved in the anti-colonial struggle from the country. Houphouët Boigny would go on to participate in all of France's dirty tricks. In North Africa, Tunisia and Morocco became independent in 1956, but Hassan II, the successor to Mohamed V, had to face the challenge of nationalist movements under Ben Barka. France would have a hand in his assassination in 1965. France still controlled the Sahara in Tunisia (which has much less oil than was believed at the time) and retained a naval base in Bizerte. In July 1961, faced with approaching Tunisian soldiers who were threatening to dismantle the Saharan oil zone, de Gaulle called in the air force and the paratroopers, causing 700 Tunisian casualties.

45. The legislative bill adopted by the French National Assembly on March 12, 1956, by 455 votes (among which the 146 members of parliament from the French Communist Party) against 76 enabled the French government in Algeria "to take all exceptional measures in view of reestablishing order, protecting persons and property, and safe-guarding the territory."

46. See Todd Shepard, *The Invention of Decolonization: The Algerian War and the Remaking of France* (Ithaca, N.Y.: Cornell University Press, 2006), revised and updated in the French translation *1962: Comment l'indépendance algérienne a transformé la France* (Paris: Payot, 2008).

47. "For a large portion of European and American publications, bolshevism was viewed as the sworn enemy, not of democracy as such, but [...] of the global white supremacy on which it relied [...]. On the other side of the Atlantic, a book taking the October Revolution as its starting point and condemning the 'rising tide of peoples of color against white world-supremacy' in its very title was met with extraordinary accolades. Once again, bolshevism was accused of being the 'moral enemy of civilization and of race,' a 'renegade' and 'traitor' to whites [...]. The author of that book received public praise from two United States presidents, Harding and Hoover." Domenico Losurdo, *Le Péché originel*, 26.

48. Jean-Raymond Tournoux, *La Tragédie du général* (Paris: Plon, 1967), 365.

49. Kirstin Ross, *May '68 and Its Afterlives* (Chicago: The University of Chicago Press, 2004).

50. "All the political currents (even those still constituting themselves) which participated in May 68 were involved in actions of solidarity" with the Vietnamese revolution, writes Pierre Rousset. In France on November 30, 1966, a particularly active National Vietnam Committee (CVN) was formed. Pierre Rousset, "La Solidarité envers les luttes indochinoises dans la 'France de 68': les années 1960–1970," [Solidarity With Indochinese Struggles in '1968 France': the 1960s and 1970s] *Europe Solidaire sans Frontières*, February 1, 2008, http://www.europe-solidaire.org/ spip.php?article9823.

4. First Racial Skirmishes in the Heart of France

51. Genet, Jean, *The Declared Enemy*, 178.

52. *Ibid*, 31.

53. This statement, published by the magazine *Le Point* on October 15, 1994, is taken from a book by Alain Peyrefitte, *Ainsi*

parlait de Gaulle. In the name of the preservation of white France, de Gaulle was opposed to the "integration" of Algeria as it was championed by the ultra-colonialists. Quoted in Thomas Deltombe, *L'Islam imaginaire. La construction de l'islamophobie médiatique, 1975–2005* (Paris: La Découverte, 2005).

54. Interview with Jacques Foccart, November 8, 1968. Quoted in Jacques Foccart, *Mémoires. Journal de l'Elysée. Tome 2: Le Général en mai, 1968–1969* (Paris: Fayard/Jeune Afrique, 1998).

55. Alexis Spire, *Étrangers à la carte: l'administration de l'immigration en France (1945–1975)* (Paris: Grasset, 2005), 112

56. Ibid., 114.

57. Patrick Weil, *Qu'est-ce qu'un français? Histoire de la nationalité française depuis la Révolution* (Paris: Grasset, 2002), 145.

58. Ibid., cited 147.

59. Ibid., 149.

60. "Undoubtedly, the implicitly ethno-cultural logic of public powers hindered any action aimed at improving housing conditions for Maghrebin immigrants, as they did not wish for them to stay long" (Ibid., 103).

61. Alexis Spire, *Étrangers à la carte*, 240.

62. John Edgar Wideman, *Brothers and Keepers* (New York: Houghton Mifflin Company, 2005 (1984)) 221.

63. Raphaël Confiant, *Nègre marron: récit* (Paris: Ecriture, 2006) note p. 59.

64. Mogniss Abdallah, *J'y suis. J'y reste! Les luttes de l'immigration depuis les années soixante* (Paris: Reflex, 2000).

65. In particular, the chronology provided in issue 25 of the journal *Migrance* published by the Générique association, third quarter of 2005.

66. Translator's note: Federation of Immigrant Workers from Black Africa, Algerian Workers Committee, Union of Tunisian

Immigrant Workers, Moroccan Workers Association, Mauritian Undocumented Immigrant Movement, Ivoirian Workers Movement, and the Immigrant Workers Home.

67. Some families would live in the *cités de transit* for twenty years.

68. Mogniss Abdallah, *J'y suis. J'y reste!*, 10.

69. "Jean-Marie Le Pen, president and candidate of the Front national, made no reference to it in the four pages and ten points that made up the platform he presented to the French people." (Patrick Weil, *Qu'est-ce qu'un Français?*, 119)

70. On July 3, 1974, the Council of Ministers decided to suspend immigration by foreign workers and their families. (Alexis Spire, *Étrangers à la carte*, 247).

72. Ibid., 253.

73. Ibid., 247. Patrick Weil, *Qu'est-ce qu'un Français?*, 165.

74. "Lee had met this kind of liberal […] and had always been frightened by them. They were the kind of white people who were honest and sincere in their regard for Negroes, who would eat and sleep with them, marry them and live with them on a social level, who might fight ceaselessly and valiantly to bring about a solution for their oppression, who might even become martyrs for their cause and bleed and die for them […]. But from beginning to end they could not accept the proposition for which they died, and could never live in equality with those for whom they had fought so heroically to have considered equal—simply because deep inside of them inequality was a fact." Chester Himes, *Lonely Crusade* (New York, Thunder's Mouth Press, 1947), 142.

75. On November 5, 1954, at the podium of the National Assembly, he declared: "The Algerian rebellion only has one final outcome: war."

76. Which is not new. However, at the end of the 1970s, this policy was all the more obvious in that it countered the predominant anti-racism of the other forces on the left. In *Les Frontières de la démocratie*, published at the time, Étienne Balibar virulently critiqued the direction taken by the PCF: "It's defense of the 'French'

worker led it into chauvinist campaigns on the theme of 'producing French,' or anti-immigration protests like the destruction of a home for immigrant workers in Vitry initiated by the communist mayor of the town (December 1980) or the denunciation of a Moroccan family (wrongly) suspected of drug trafficking by the communist mayor of Montigny-les-Corneilles (Val-d'Oise), Robert Hue (February 1981)." "The (Communist) Party borrowed Stoleru's language and his slogan to immediately stop immigration—while at the same time offering him the prime role as 'defender of immigrants,' really adding insult to injury—without specifying any conditions that would allow action or expression by immigrants themselves, even though they knew that this watchword was used in practice to justify arbitrary deportations" (Étienne Balibar, *Les Frontières de la démocratie* (Paris: La Découverte, 1981), 30). For his part, Deltombe describes the hostility of the PCF against the building of mosques. In Rennes, for example, the communists, who wanted to confront the socialist mayor of the city, claimed that the financial aid for the mosque was "not in line with the republican tradition of separation of church and state or with the social and cultural interests of French and immigrant workers." For its part, the PS denounced the "so-called dogmatic antireligious secularism" of the communists and gave its definition of secularity: "It consists of respecting differences and giving each person the possibility of living their culture" (Deltombe, *Islam imaginaire*, 48).

5. From Marronage to Jihad: The Metamorphoses of Indigenous Power

77. Translator's note: The neologism "beur," formed by reversing the syllables of the French word for Arab (*arabe*), is used to refer to a person born in France to one or more parents who immigrated from North Africa, in particular the Maghreb.

78. Abdelmalek Sayad, *Les enfants illégitimes*, 19.

79. Idem.

80. Ibid., 16.

81. I am not talking about those who joined these parties as a career choice, benefitting from the "*beur*" wave just as some today are

taking advantage of the issue of "diversity," but those who, even today, think they are capable of doing something there to benefit the populations of immigrant origin. It is also true that, sometimes, personal ambition and sincere conviction can blend together. The same could be said of the indigenous who joined associations like SOS-Racisme. While, at the time, in the heat of the polemics often raised by real issues, radical militants could rightly denounce those who demeaned themselves in these movements, we cannot in hindsight, and in a broader historical perspective, see all of these militants who tried this type of experience as opportunists and traitors. While some of them were, there were also sincere militants.

82. See the book by Lilian Mathieu, *La Double Peine. Histoire d'une lutte inachevée* (Paris: La Dispute, 2006).

83. This association was established by Mohamed Hocine who himself fought a long battle to dismiss a deportation order given to him after a prison sentence. See the interview he gave in *L'Indigène de la République* 8 (June 2007).

84. See http://lmsi.net/

85. Esther Benbasa and Jean-Christophe Artias, *Juifs et musulmans. Une histoire partagée, un dialogue à construire* (Paris: La Découverte, 2006), 7.

86. The unctuous Jean Daniel is the very prototype of the leftist colonialist. A quote in passing: "What I personally have called the 'crime' of Le Pen is obviously not his discussion of the 'normal' issues of security and immigration. On the contrary, and precisely, by poisoning the debates on these questions, he has made those claimed to face them feel guilty. For fear of helping Le Pen, Valéry Giscard d'Estaing had to withdraw the word 'invasion,' Jacques Chirac apologized for mentioning 'odors,' Laurent Fabius lamented saying that Le Pen was giving bad answers to good questions, Michel Rocard passed his time correcting the simple observation that France cannot accept all the misery of the world, and Édouard Balladur regretted calling for 'national preference.' This hardly means that I find all these statements appropriate, and I vehemently fought against some of them, but they came from politicians who were by no means racist and should have led to national debate." (Jean Daniel, *Le Nouvel Observateur*, April 24, 2003).

87. Ernest Renan, *La Réforme intellectuelle et morale* (1871).

88. Translator's note: "*souchiens*" is a neologism referring to an imagined "original" or "native" French, "*Français de souche*."

89. In *La Traite silencieuse. Les émigrés des Dom* (Paris: IDOC, 1975), cited by Claude-Valentin Marie, "Les Antillais en France: la nouvelle donne," *Hommes et Migration* 1237 (May-June 2002).

90. Ibid., 35. ("Antilleans, Guyanese, Reunionese, in action let's take what we demand.")

91. Ibid., 36.

92. See my book, *Pour une politique de la racaille* (Paris: Textuel, 2006), in particular the documents produced by the MIR available on its website (http://www.indigenes-republique.fr/) and in its monthly *L'indigène de la République*.

6. How the Strategic Unity of White Power Was Built

93. In addition, and increasingly today, new constraints were placed on the former colonies to have them bear the burden of limiting emigration.

94. Patrick Weil notes that "the dissenting votes in the second reading did not call into question the fundamental agreement: they were only due to the political effect caused by the score of the Front National in the European elections." In other words, the right was indulging in electoral one-upmanship but the consensus was fundamentally well-established (Patrick Weil, *Qu'est-ce qu'un français?*, 286.

95. Ibid., 289.

96. Saïd Bonamama explains it very well in his book *Dix ans de marche des Beurs. Chronique d'un movement avorté* (Paris: Desclée de Brouwer, 1994).

97. Wole Soyinka, "Nobel Lecture 1986: This Past Must Address Its Present," *PMLA* 102, 5 (October 1987), 762–771.

98. April 9, 1986. Cited by Lilian Mathieu, *La Double Peine*, 139.

99. The reform of the Nationality Code established choice for the acquisition of French nationality for young people born in France of foreign parents and restricts jus solis. From now on, "a child born of foreign parents shall—between the age of 16 to 21—manifest the intention to be French, instead of French nationality being automatically granted on reaching adulthood. [...] as for acquisition by marriage, the law passed from then on required the spouse of a French citizen to wait two years instead of six months to become French by declaration. Finally, a significant obstacle, a child born in France of a parent born in Algeria before 1962 would not receive French nationality from birth—due to a double jus solis effect—unless this parent shows proof that they have held residence in France for more at least 5 years" (Patrick Weil, *Qu'est-ce qu'un français?*, 176).

100. "The new legislation adopted in 1998 attempted to implement a synthesis between the principle of equal access to French nationality (established by the Law of 1889) and the requirement of freedom of choice (reinforced in 1993). The principle of equality was reasserted, since the law provides that at the age of 18, any child born in France of a foreign parent is French, if they still reside in France and as long as they lived their during their adolescence. The existing requirement of five years could be discontinuous between the age of 11 to 18. [...] However, the freedom of choice of the child is respected more. The power of parents to declare children French during their childhood without their consent was not reestablished [...]. In the six months prior to the eighteenth birthday and especially in the year that follows, when they have reached adulthood, the adolescent can declare whether they wish to remain foreign and decline the quality of being French. Finally, starting from the age of 13 to 18 years old, they can anticipate state recognition of their quality as French and manifest the intention to be French (with parental authorization between 13 and 16 years old)" (Ibid., 181).

101. *Le Figaro-magazine*, September 21, 1991.

102. According to Rémy Leveau and Catherine Wihtol de Wenden, the hidden thread of the controversies that accompanied the Chalandon reform could be resumed in a single question: "How can one be French and Muslim?" Rémy Leveau and

Catherine Wihtol de Wenden, *La Beurgeoisie. Les trois âges de la vie associative issue de l'immigration* (Paris: CNRS éditions, 2001), 65.

103. One avowal among others, the column by Alain Juppé titled "We may not be able to avoid conflict with Islam." *Libération*, November 29, 2004.

104. Thomas Deltombe, *L'Islam imaginaire*, 50. The reference to Shiism was obviously inspired by the Iranian Revolution. The events in the Middle East had direct repercussions in France where they fed Islamophobia. As such, the involvement of French troops starting in September 1982 in the context of a "multinational force" stationed in Lebanon had immediate implications: kidnapping of French citizens and successive attacks in Paris and Marseille. Palestinian and Lebanese Muslims were presented as terrible barbarians against whom the Christians of Lebanon and the state of Israel were defending themselves as best they could.

105. "Sept sur Sept" program on the channel TF1, December 3, 1989, cited in Thomas Deltombe, *L'Islam imaginaire*, 118.

106. Presidential speech on channel TF1, Antenne 2, December 10, 1989, cited in Thomas Deltombe, *L'Islam imaginaire*, 118.

107. Journal de 20 heures [8pm news], channel TF1, December 8, 1989, cited in Thomas Deltombe, *L'Islam imaginaire*, 118.

108. Wave of attacks in the mid-1990s.

109. October 25, 1994, cited in Thomas Deltombe, *L'Islam imaginaire*, 230.

110. Frantz Fanon, *The Wretched of the Earth* (New York: Grove/Atlantic, 2004 (1963)), p. 108.

111. Thomas Deltombe, *L'Islam imaginaire*, 205.

112. Ibid., 244.

113. At the start of the 2003 school year, the two students were expelled by the disciplinary council of the Lycée d'Aubervilliers

because they refused to remove their veils. The polemic on the veil had been relaunched by the government on the right since May and June of the same year in the context of a strong strike movement against retirement reform. The PS also joined in: Jack Lang proposed a bill to prohibit the wearing of "scarves" at school. For his part, on May 18, before the PS Congress in Dijon, Laurent Fabius defended the prohibition on "ostentatious religious signs" in schools and public spaces.

114. The law on secularity passed in March 2004 prohibited the wearing of any "ostentatious" religious signs in school.

115. Esther Benbassa, for her part, notes the influence of the Napoleonian model of institutionalization of a form of representation of French Jews.

116. Aziz Zemmouri and Vincent Geisser, *Marianne et Allah. Les politiques français face à la "question muslumane"* (Paris: La Découverte, 2007), 82.

117. Ibid., 26.

118. LMSI chronology.

119. Ibid.

120. The LSQ was passed on November 15, 2001.

121. "Ripostes" program, channel France 5, 2002.

122. Contrary to what it claims, the parliamentary left first approved the law of February 23. For the conditions of its adoption and the reactions it elicited, see Romain Bertrand, *Mémoires d'empire. La controverse autour du "fait colonial"* (Paris: éditions du Croquant, 2006). While the analyses proposed in the second half of the book are highly debatable, in particular concerning the positions of the Movement of the Indigenous of the Republic, the book is nonetheless full of useful information.

123. It was the law of 2001 "recognizing the slave trade and slavery from the fifteenth to the nineteenth centuries as a crime against humanity."

7. Working-Class Neighborhoods

124. It should be noted, however, that a sudden influx of "barbarians" in a wealthy neighborhood immediately causes phenomena of rejection. For example, the protests by inhabitants and merchants in the Marais neighborhood of Paris, concerned by the increasing number of workshops and shops run by Chinese.

125. Gérard Noiriel is a necessary reference for European immigration policies. However, for this historian full of illusion for the Republic, the question of contemporary indigenousness is out of reach.

126. "Algerian families elicit even greater attention from municipal administrations in that they solicit them directly. A report submitted in 1964 by representatives of the municipal welfare office showed that there was not one position on which these families did not weigh. In the school offices and in the social-medical services financed by the municipality, in particular in the maternal and child protection (PMI) centers, students and families of Maghrebin origin received the most municipal assistance" (Olivier Masclet, *La Gauche et les cités. Enquête sur un rendez-vous manqué* (Paris: La Dispute, 2003), 36). Which led to demands that wealthier towns also take charge of immigrants.

127. In fact, the mobilization of PCF towns against immigrants began to be put in place in the 1950s.

128. A few months after May 1968, more precisely in October, a decree was published by the government requiring housing project organizations to reserve a third of their units for those in inadequate housing. The state, which progressively withdrew from social housing assistance, therefore required red cities to house immigrants but also forced them to carry the budgetary load. "Starting in 1968 and the imposition of a quota of households listed in prefectural records for 'inadequate housing' on social housing (HLM) offices, rehousing in social housing became more frequent. Yet while the hopes of families grew, not all were rehoused in the same way. As Daniel Lalande indicates, the prefecture established an order of priority that reflects, if not the racist ideas of state agents, at least their representation of the 'assimilability' of immigrant families. The rehoused families were first Spanish, then Portuguese, then Tunisian. Last were

the Algerian families whose establishment in France was therefore strongly discouraged" (Olivier Masclet, *La Gauche et les cités*, 47).

129. Cited by Olivier Masclet, "Du 'bastion' au 'ghetto.' Le communisme municipal en butte à l'immigration," *Actes de la recherche en sciences sociales* 159 (September 2005), 22.

130. Olivier Masclet, *La Gauche et les cités*, 50.

131. The increased visibility of immigrants is expressed notably in their occupation of the housing space. Restricted until then to factories and shantytowns, starting in the mid-1970s: "From 1975 to 1990, foreign households living in precarious housing went from 10% to 4%. For Algerians, the departure from furnished lodgings seemed spectacular: in 15 years, 70% of households gained access to other types of housing, in particular the social housing stock. This process of diffusion was also seen with other Maghrebin populations" (Patrick Simon, *Les Discriminaitons raciales et ethniques dans l'accès au logement social*, GELD note 3, Paris (2001)). The diffusion of immigrants, for whom family reunification had already started in the 1960s, developed in the 1970s in the least attractive segments of the social housing stock. In the mid-1980s, the Socialist government decided to eliminate transitional housing and rehouse their occupants. It resulted in great pressure from the state on public and private social housing organizations so that they could house immigrants coming from these housing projects.

132. Olivier Masclet, *La Gauche et les cités*, 77.

133. Ibid., 89.

134. "Made to connect to the status of the person bearing it, it can only in this specific case suffer the depreciation from which this same person suffers: this borrowed attribute is only socially speaking the nationality of a naturalized (Algerian) immigrant, a discount nationality" (Abdelmalek Sayad, "Les immigrés algériens et la nationalité française," in *Questions de nationalité. Histoire et enjeux d'un code*, under the direction of Smaïn Laacher (Paris: CIEMI-L'Harmattan, 1987), 142).

135. Sylvie Tissot, "Une 'discrimination informelle'? Usages du concept de mixité sociale dans la gestion des attributions de logements HLM," *Actes de la recherche en sciences sociales* 159 (September 2005),

69. See also by the same author : *L'État et les quartiers. Genèse d'une catégorie de l'action politique* (Paris: Seuil, 2007).

136. Frantz Fanon, *The Wretched of the Earth*, p. 4–5.

8. A New Phase in the Colonial Counter-Revolution

137. Fight against retirement reform in 2003, massive victory of the "no" vote on the proposed European constitution in 2005, and vast mobilization against the CPE (first employment contract) in 2006, among others.

138. Headed by the French Socialist Dominique Strauss-Kahn!

139. Frantz Fanon, *The Wretched of the Earth*, 53.

140. From this perspective, see the brilliant analysis proposed by Israeli anti-Zionist Yitzhak Laor of the sudden importance of the commemoration of the genocide of the Jews in Europe and the assimilation between Muslims and anti-Semites in his essay *The Myths of Liberal Zionism* (New York: Verso, 2017) (French title: *Le Nouveau philosémitisme européen et "le camp de la paix" en Israël* (Paris: Éditions La Fabrique, 2007).

141. Balibar, *Race, Nation, Class*, p. 43.

142. René Gallissot, *Misère de l'anti-racisme* (Paris: Arcantère éditions, 1985), 54.

Heading into the Waves...

143. Jean Genet, "Letter to American Intellectuals," *The Declared Enemy*, 31.

144. James Baldwin, *The Evidence of Things Not Seen*, 6–7.

145. See also the passionate essay by Raphaël Confiant where, while celebrating the anti-colonialist Aimé Césaire, he asks whether Césaire "was not in a way a hostage of the mulatto class" (Raphaël Confiant, *Aimé Césaire. Une traverse paradoxale du siècle* (Montreal: Éditions Écriture, 2006 (1993)), 84.

146. Patrick Chamoiseau, *Slave Old Man* (New York: The New Press, 2018 (1997)).

Sadri Khiari holds a doctorate in political science. A member of the Tunisian democratic opposition, he currently lives in France.